Beyond the Male Idol Factory

Asian Celebrity and Fandom Studies

Asia arguably has the world's most vibrant star, celebrity and fandom cultures, due in part to its globalized entertainment media and cultural industries and its large population base, and yet there is little sustained scholarship on this highly significant cultural and economic arena. *The Asian Celebrity and Fandom Studies Series* aims to meet this research gap, promoting new and innovative scholarship in Asian media and cultural studies, and screen studies, by concentrating on the most salient issues surrounding Asian stardom, celebrity and fandom.

The Asian Celebrity and Fandom Studies Series is devoted to the publication of scholarly books that critically examine star, celebrity and fandom cultures in specific Asian countries, in trans-Asian or trans-national contexts, and among Asian diasporas. The series publishes monographs, co-authored books and edited collections. All proposal and manuscripts are subject to rigorous peer review.

Published Titles:

Boys Love Media in Thailand: Celebrity, Fans, and Transnational Asian Queer Popular Culture by Thomas Baudinette
Contemporary Chinese Celebrities: Moral Transgressions, Rights Defence and Public Concerns by Shenshen Cai
Beyond the Male Idol Factory: The Construction of Gender and National Ideologies in Japan through Johnny's Jimusho by Yunuen Ysela Mandujano-Salazar

Forthcoming Titles:

Livestreaming China: An Ethnography of Vulgar Boredom by Dino Ge Zhang

Series Editors: Jian Xu and Sean Redmond

Beyond the Male Idol Factory

*The Construction of Gender and National
Ideologies in Japan through Johnny's Jimusho*

Yunuen Ysela Mandujano-Salazar

BLOOMSBURY ACADEMIC
LONDON · NEW YORK · OXFORD · NEW DELHI · SYDNEY

BLOOMSBURY ACADEMIC
Bloomsbury Publishing Plc, 50 Bedford Square, London, WC1B 3DP, UK
Bloomsbury Publishing Inc, 1359 Broadway, 12th Floor, New York, NY 10018, USA
Bloomsbury Publishing Ireland, 29 Earlsfort Terrace, Dublin 2, D02 AY28, Ireland

BLOOMSBURY, BLOOMSBURY ACADEMIC and the Diana logo are
trademarks of Bloomsbury Publishing Plc

First published in Great Britain 2024
This paperback edition published 2026

Series design: Ben Anslow
Cover image © VCG / Contributor / Getty Images

A catalogue record for this book is available from the British Library.

A catalog record for this book is available from the Library of Congress.

ISBN: HB: 978-1-3503-5978-9
PB: 978-1-3503-5982-6
ePDF: 978-1-3503-5980-2
eBook: 978-1-3503-5979-6

Series: Asian Celebrity and Fandom Studies

Typeset by Integra Software Services Pvt. Ltd.

For product safety related questions contact productsafety@bloomsbury.com.

To find out more about our authors and books visit www.bloomsbury.com
and sign up for our newsletters.

To the idols for inspiring thousands of people,
including me.
To the fans who shared their experiences
over the years.

Contents

Figures

Tables

Acknowledgements

The research behind this book was conducted at diverse stages due to the financial support of The Japan Foundation, the University Autonomous of Ciudad Juarez (UACJ) and Mexico's National Council of Science and Technology (CONACyT). I want to express my gratitude to these institutions, as well as to Jason Karlin and Hiroshi Aoyagi who guided me when I was conducting my doctoral dissertation, which was part of the basis for this product.

Note on translation

This book relies on vast sources in the Japanese language, which were analysed directly by the author. In explaining the diverse topics, the author made the translations respecting the original sense and style. However, when it was considered that translating them would make them lose some original meaning, the terms are presented in Romanized Japanese. This book follows the romanization system of the *Kenkyusha's New Japanese-English Dictionary* (3rd and later) for general terminology. In the case of Japanese names, the surname appears first, followed by the given name, except in the case of Johnny Kitagawa, who is mentioned following the Western order by Japanese media. The romanization for celebrities' names, products, companies, institutions and shows follows the style presented by Japanese media, without macron (ˉ). Finally, for Japanese cities and regions, the romanization follows that of the *Oxford English Dictionary*.

Introduction

A week in the – media – life of Arashi

March 2018. Two months after finishing their national tour *Untitled,* in which around 855,000 people attended eighteen concerts, this was the weekly schedule for Arashi's members on national television.

Monday, 11.00 pm. Sakurai Sho presents the latest political information at Nippon Television (NTV)'s *News Zero,* formally dressed in a black suit, white shirt and black tie. He returned two weeks before from Pyeongchang, where he was one of the newscasters covering the 2018 Winter Olympics.

Thursday, 7.00 pm. Fuji Television (Fuji TV) broadcasts Arashi's weekly variety show *VS Arashi.* Dressed in sweatpants, jeans and t-shirts, the five members compete with a guest team in air hockey.

Thursday, 10.00 pm. Tokyo Broadcasting System (TBS) broadcasts Sakurai Sho's weekly variety show *Sakurai Ariyoshi THE Yakai.* Dressed in a grey suit, black shirt and red tie, Sakurai is joking while interviewing a young actress who is that day's guest.

Friday, 9.00 pm. Arashi is a guest at Asahi Television (Asahi TV)'s *Music Station,* a weekly music show. The five members wear casual jeans and colourful shirts while dancing and singing their latest single, *Find The Answer,* which is the theme song for Matsumoto's series *99.9 Season 2.*

Friday, 12.00 am. Aiba Masaki is at Bunka Hōsō transmitting his weekly radio show *Aiba Masaki no Recomen! Arashi Remix.*

Saturday, 7.00 pm. NTV broadcasts *Shimura dōbutsuen,* a weekly family variety show in which Aiba Masaki is one of the main hosts. Dressed in a white t-shirt and denim overall, he plays with a baby lion at some zoo.

Saturday, 9.00 pm. NTV broadcasts Arashi's weekly variety show *Arashi ni Shiyagare*. The five members are dressed in shirts and jeans and are playing a quiz game to win the chance to taste some food.

Sunday, 10.25 am. NTV broadcasts Ninomiya Kazunari's weekly variety show *Nino-san*. Dressed casually, he laughs at the comments of one of the comedians at the show.

Sunday, 6.00 pm. TV Asahi broadcasts Aiba Masaki's weekly variety show *Aiba Manabu*. Dressed in jeans and a t-shirt, he cooks in an open-air improvised kitchen.

Sunday, 9.00 pm. TBS broadcasts Matsumoto Jun's detective series *99.9 Season 2*. He is starring as a criminal lawyer.

Sunday, 9.50 pm. Nippon Hōsō Kyōkai (NHK) broadcasts the weekly sports show *Sunday Sports*. Aiba Masaki, one of the main hosts, is dressed in sweatpants and a white t-shirt and tries to imitate the moves of football shown by the guest, one of the stars of Japan's National Team.

Sunday, 10.00 pm. Ninomiya Kazunari is at Bayfm transmitting his weekly radio show *BAY STORM*.

Besides these activities, the five idols made diverse guest appearances at other variety shows to promote their own. Furthermore, their faces appeared in numerous advertisements for cars, insurance, snacks, soft drinks, beers, medicine, housing, videogames on television and spectacular billboards.

The nation of idols

Japan is a country full of images. Particularly in cities, one can barely escape from the smiling faces of celebrities who announce everything imaginable, from products to public services. Those faces may look almost the same for people unfamiliar with Japanese media culture, and the advertising may not differ much from that in other contemporary societies. However, for the residents of Japan, some of the faces shown everywhere have a deeper meaning than just the products they are promoting. Such is the case of male idols generally called 'Johnny's', the multi-talent celebrities produced by the company known as Johnny's Jimusho. With origins in the 1960s, this company has grown to be the most powerful talent agency in Japan, having a solid grip over media corporations that depend on its idols to attract audiences and sell advertising.

Since the turn of the century, groups produced by Johnny's Jimusho have been recurrently referred to as national idols. As shown in the previous section by the typical media schedule of one of these groups, these idols are in very different types of content and aim at diverse audiences and interests. They are not only singers, dancers or actors; they do almost everything and appear every day, in one way or another, in front of Japanese society.

Despite the relevance in Japan of the company and its idols, there is very little academic literature about them, mainly because Johnny's Jimusho is very protective of its idols and business model and does not allow outsiders to get direct interviews or images. This situation was evidenced in March 2023, while I was writing this book. Johnny's Jimusho attracted international attention because the British Broadcasting Corporation (BBC) released a documentary about Johnny Kitagawa – the founder of the talent agency – who two decades before had been involved in allegations of sexual abuse against some of the teenage idols in his company. During the hour-long documentary, the reporter expressed numerous times his surprise about the difficulties of getting information regardless of this being such an important company in Japan and such serious allegations.

Thus, this book aims to provide one step forward in the comprehension of the male idol industry inside Japan. The analysis presented is located within the intersection of the cultural, media, celebrity and fan studies, and relies on theories of cultural nationalism and gender ideologies. I followed a qualitative approach using documentary analysis and traditional and digital ethnography to obtain vast and variated information from diverse aspects of the phenomenon; and applied interpretative textual analysis to deconstruct and reconstruct the history of the company, the production process of the idols, the ideologies they embody and represent, as well as their meaning for Japanese fans.

Celebrities in contemporary societies

The importance of media culture in contemporary societies should not be ignored or underestimated. The influential power that some media products achieve makes them essential in the political, economic and ideological strategies of the powers and governments in the mediation within their societies and with others. Moreover, the intertextuality of media culture induces people to accept the dominant ideologies by presenting them consistently through many forms, supporting the naturalization of those ideas. Nonetheless, although media culture, mainly that produced by mainstream media, conveys the ideology of the dominant sectors of a society, it cannot become prevalent unless it shows elements that the audiences recognize and accept (Fiske 2005). Barthes (1977, 1999) proposed that any cultural representation could support the establishment of myths: the ideological process that allows the dominant discourse to become common sense.

In this process, celebrities are one of the main ideological escapes that elites use to interpellate people and negotiate with society, trying to establish hegemonic ideologies; but, they will only attain that role if people recognize themselves in the values and identities represented by the media idols. The expansion of media in societies has made celebrities a widespread symbol or totem of the practices and ideologies of the society that produces them. Because their symbolism is rebuilt incessantly by the producers and the audiences, they are an updated representation of the dominant ideologies. Celebrities are sometimes underestimated for their shallowness and commodification. Indeed, they do not have the virtues of the heroes of other times; they are media products built on the familiarity of their images and personalities. As Boorstin (1992) rightly denounced, they are made to comfort and comply with the audiences' tastes. Nevertheless, in contemporary societies, this is why they are one of the most powerful tools by which people make sense of the world; they are images and narratives that circulate unceasingly through media and are consumed with enthusiasm. For such reason, Marshall (1997: 65) said that a media personality's power in society derives directly from the audience because celebrities 'represent subject positions that audiences can adopt or adapt in their formation of social identities. [… They are] an embodiment of a discursive battleground on the norms of individuality and personality within a culture'. Hence, the presence and media power that achieve certain celebrities and the discourses they represent should be understood as the result of the constant negotiation among the agents involved in their production and circulation, including the audience.

In the twentieth-first century, the study of celebrities has become an interdisciplinary academic field on its own, using approaches from cultural and media studies, as well as sociology, anthropology and other disciplines

(Holmes and Redmond 2010). Celebrities are texts in the meta-reality or a midpoint between reality and fiction built by media intertextuality. The intersection of celebrities with other texts and the socially situated reader activates the discourse of what they represent (Lukács 2010). Also, people's acceptance or rejection of celebrities is not an entirely rational process in which people consciously agree or reject the ideology they represent; audiences feel attracted or repelled by them and, consequently, accept or reject their symbolic package. This emotional reaction is transformed into an affective power that impacts how well the text that is a celebrity circulates (Grossberg 2001; Karlin 2012; Marshall 1997). The impact of the emotional response is powerful; a celebrity that causes positive responses may influence people's actions or thoughts significantly, but if pushed too far, that affection can turn into hatred and result in an aversion to everything that the celebrity represents. To encourage a positive affective power, producers constantly play with the balance of the binaries of ordinary-extraordinary, idealization-familiarity and characterization-realism that are at the base of the symbolic construction of any celebrity (Lukács 2010). In the case of celebrities known as idols, the relationship developed with the fans – the core consumers – is 'intimate and intense, deeply affecting and moving, simultaneously both personal and shared' (Aoyagi, Galbraith and Kovacic 2021: 2).

Regardless of the importance of celebrities in contemporary societies and the growing field of celebrity studies, most of the literature focuses on the analysis of European and American cases. On the other hand, Asia's presence in global affairs is growing, and its diversity of vibrant media and celebrities' cultures offers contexts worth studying; numerous under-researched phenomena can allow for innovative theoretical and methodological approaches (Xu, Donnar and Kishore 2021). Such is the motivation behind this book, to offer a comprehensive and interdisciplinary analysis of an under-researched case of celebrities that dominate Japan's landscape: male idols produced by Johnny's Jimusho.

The Japanese context and the research on idols

Although all countries constantly work to reinforce the national identity in their societies, the mediums and discourses differ according to the context and threats they face. In the case of Japan, nationalism and patriotism have been regularly found in its historical development, with ideologies endorsed by the government as complex policies related to education, military and industry. Fiske (2005) said that when there is an attempt to produce or defend a national culture through media, the middle-class tastes and definitions of culture and nation tend to dominate. In Japan, during the postwar period, public and commercial television played a crucial role in rebuilding and maintaining a sense of national community based on the ideological foundations of a national middle-class society through the images and messages of socially realistic productions (Lukács 2010; Vogel 1971). However, in the 1990s, there was a break in the mass-consumer imaginary; to appeal to the diversifying identities of young generations, individual tastes and preferences, a high stratification of market targets was the new normal in all industries, including media.

Nevertheless, producers of all types of goods and services, the government and diverse public and private groups of interest continued relying on media and celebrities to sell their products or represent their ideas. However, producers more carefully crafted the celebrities' images to serve these aims and reach meticulously defined audiences. In the twentieth-first century, the daily lives of Japan's residents have been invaded by obvious but somehow soft patriotic messages about Japanese people's harmony, strength and future. One crucial element in this campaign is the idol industry. Japanese idols are celebrities who provide entertainment and act as role models to society. Since the emergence of this kind of celebrity, during the rapid economic growth period of the 1960s, idols have been a lucrative media product that has evolved into a robust industry within Japanese entertainment and a persuasive device to convey ideologies from the power institutions to society.

Despite this phenomenon's importance for a greater understanding of diverse social aspects of contemporary Japan, there are still limited studies about it. Essential works are Galbraith's (2021), Karlin's (2012) and Marx's (2012), which analyse aspects of the entertainment system in Japan and the production of certain types of idols and celebrities; also, Aoyagi and Kovacic's (2021), which advanced a theoretical approach on the symbolism of all types of idols and their capacity to transform fan practices into rituals. Aoyagi's (2005) ethnographic work is fundamental because it presents a detailed analysis of the production process in the 1980s and 1990s and how the industry absorbed female teenagers and transformed them into specific personas to be marketed and to contribute to the construction of other teenagers' ideal self-images. Next, Sakai (2005) reviews the history of the emergence of idols as opposed to stars, which are celebrities with other symbolic characteristics and dominated Japanese entertainment in the decades before 1970; he also ponders the role that idols play as symbolic goods in Japanese international politics. Finally, Galbraith (2012, 2018) explores the production, circulation and politics behind AKB48, a famous female idol group; he analyses how the discourses and representations of the group echo a national identity and how they are consumed.

On the other hand, much less has been written in the category of male idols, which Johnny's Jimusho has mostly monopolized for six decades. A few works, like those of Darling-Wolf (2004) and Nagaike (2012), discussed the role of specific male idol groups in the construction of female fantasies about masculine ideals. Furthermore, in previous works, I have explored, through one of Johnny's group's representation and narratives, the national and gender ideologies that are being circulated in contemporary Japanese society (Mandujano 2014a; Mandujano-Salazar 2009, 2014a, 2016, 2018a, 2018b, 2020). Nonetheless, in the context of the growing popularity of Asian idols across the globe, this book is the first effort to present a comprehensive academic analysis of the male idols in contemporary Japan in the English language.

Origins and methodology

Debord (1977) said, in his critical work *The Society of the Spectacle*, that the spectacle was a world view and a social relationship mediated by images; he stressed that to analyse it, one should talk its language. The researcher must deeply understand the context in which the cultural phenomenon of interest is produced and how the average person makes sense of it. Therefore, the researcher should do a continuous emic-etic exercise and try to obtain as many readings as possible from members of the society to be analysed. Considering this, the present book is based on twenty years of research on diverse aspects of

Johnny's Jimusho and its idols and my experience as a Japanese Studies scholar. It builds on my Master's and Doctoral dissertations and previous publications to analyse the phenomenon systematically and from diverse perspectives.

I lived in Japan between 2005 and 2006, and, at that time, I was impressed by the popularity that Johnny's idols had with teenagers and adults and by the longevity of their careers. Until then, I was familiar only with the Mexican and American media and found Johnny's idols and their multi-talent and pervasiveness in media something very different and exciting. Hence, intending to understand how Johnny's idols became a prevalent media product in Japan, I began the first formal stage of research and critical analysis on Johnny's Jimusho between 2007 and 2009 during the Master's programme in Japanese Studies at El Colegio de Mexico. At this stage, the objective was to examine the company's strategies to develop a product – an idol group – and the market for it. During the summer of 2008, I conducted fieldwork in Tokyo and Sapporo, collecting media information, attending concerts and interviewing fans to understand how these idols were produced and promoted. I also collected quantitative indicators to measure the reception of the idols, such as the number of releases of singles, albums, concerts, plays, television and radio programmes, sales and ratings, and popularity surveys in magazines and official websites. After watching hours of Japanese television and reading dozens of idol and music magazines, I became interested in understanding their social and cultural implications in Japan. Although it was not the objective at that moment, I identified some trends in the narratives regarding Arashi, the most successful group during those years. In 2009, when I finished writing that thesis, the media was beginning to call Arashi *kokuminteki aidoru* (national idol) and the members were involved in governmental campaigns to promote Japan inside and outside the country.

By the spring of 2011, while applying to a doctoral programme, I noticed that after the Great East Japan Earthquake, there had been an increment in the use of Arashi in media content with narratives about the attractiveness and richness of Japan and the strength of its people. Thus, I decided to continue researching Johnny's idols, focusing on their representations and narratives to unveil the discourses they promoted towards their society. On this aim, I did two periods of fieldwork, one of six months in Tokyo in 2012; and another of eight months, between 2013 and 2014, in Osaka, through The Japan Foundation's Japanese

Language Program for Specialists in Cultural and Academic Fields. During these months, I applied traditional and digital ethnographic techniques, including participant and direct observation, semi-structured interviews and casual conversations, and the analysis of diverse digital platforms where fans interacted. I also collected information through official and non-official media and products related to Johnny's idols. All the information was coded into relevant categories and analysed with the software *Nvivo*, then reconstructed through interpretative textual analysis to advance the meaning of idols and their role in Japanese society.

After finishing this project, I continued to be interested in media discourses on Japanese and gender identity and the role of Johnny's idols in propagating them. Thus, as part of postdoctoral research, with funding from The Japan Foundation's Short-Term Fellowship Program, I went for two months to Tokyo to update and expand my information, specifically in the context of the preparations for the 2020 Tokyo Olympic Games. After that, I went back every six months, until December 2019, for about three weeks each time. On all those occasions, I observed and talked to fans and collected updated information on the idols.

Outline

The book is divided into five chapters that intend to provide a comprehensive understanding of Johnny's idols and their symbolic and ideological relevance in Japan. Chapter 1 presents the historical and sociocultural context of the emergence of Johnny's Jimusho. Relying primarily on documentary analysis, it briefly reviews the development of a cultural nationalist movement in postwar Japan and the media's role in propagating national discourses. Next, it presents crucial concepts to understand the development of Japanese media and idol culture. Finally, it reconstructs the history of Johnny's Jimusho, focusing on critical moments until it became Japan's most important producer of male idols.

Chapter 2 is a revised and updated English version of the work done for my master's thesis (Mandujano-Salazar 2009). Interestingly, when I wrote it, I selected Arashi as the most representative group of Johnny's Jimusho without knowing that it would also become representative of Japanese entertainment. The chapter follows a documentary analysis of statistics from the Recording Industry Association of Japan and other public sources of the Japanese music and entertainment industry, as well as information from Johnny's Jimusho official website and fan clubs to explore the production process of Johnny's idols. It also demonstrates, through the results of participant observation, interviews with Japanese fans, and the textual analysis of idols' media productions, the way in which ordinary teenagers become beloved idols of a whole nation, influencing various markets and industries.

Chapter 3 examines the development of Johnny's national idols stressing the discursive and representational characteristics of the groups given such labels and how they relate to a broader discourse about national identity, which intensifies in moments of national crises or distress. This chapter is based on a documentary and textual analysis of the media content of three of Johnny's groups: SMAP, Arashi and King & Prince. The section of Arashi is an extended and updated version of some previously published works based on my doctoral research (Mandujano 2014a; Mandujano-Salazar 2014, 2016, 2018b, 2020).

Chapter 4 analyses the media representations and narratives of Johnny's idols regarding gender and social expectations in twentieth-first-century Japan. Firstly, it presents the masculinity model portrayed by the idols, which is built around physical attractiveness, strength and work ethics. Then, it shows how, through their narratives and the fictional roles they portray, the idols nurture the imagination of the fans to fulfil ideal social roles, like boyfriend, lover, son and co-worker. To conclude, this chapter explores representations that appear to contradict heteronormativity but are meant to reinforce the idols' appeal to female fans.

The purpose of Chapter 5 is to present the other side of the Japanese male idol industry: the fans and their practices of consumption. It relies on traditional and digital ethnography to reconstruct essential aspects of Johnny's idols' fan culture like the sacralization of places and objects and the rituals fans perform. It also shows how fans are devoted to their idols and the ways in which the producers exploit this devotion.

The book closes with an epilogue that problematizes the cultural meaning of Johnny's idols in Japan and the recent scandal regarding the allegations of sexual abuse against Johnny Kitagawa. It also advances an interpretation of the minimal engagement of fans in this scandal, in contrast with their strong reaction to power structures and changes inside the company, which may promote the end of the monopoly of Johnny's Jimusho in Japan's male idol industry.

Media, entertainment and idols as reflections of Japan's socioeconomic transitions

Japan has a long list of art and entertainment products that have expressed the social and gender ideals of the time. Before Japan was a modern nation-state, artistic expressions such as the noh or kabuki theatre had been arenas for ideological negotiation between the elites and the society. In the first half of the twentieth century, with the arrival of the first mass media technology, Japanese elites promoted gender ideals and artists created movies and animation that reflected the social anxieties and expectations of a rapidly modernizing nation. Then, in postwar Japan, the media and entertainment industry centred on television and music, which were implanted with ideologies that would guide the new ideals for Japanese people.

This chapter presents the historical context of the emergence of Johnny's Jimusho as part of developing the entertainment industry in twentieth-century Japan until it became the country's most renowned and influential talent agency, specializing in producing male idols. It also establishes a theoretical background and critical basis for examining the ideological role that media, particularly entertainment, has in configuring Japanese national and gender ideologies.

Media and ideologies on nation and gender

Gellner (1983: 111) noted that 'the most violent phase of nationalism is that which accompanies early industrialism'. Such was the situation of Japan from 1867 until its defeat in the Pacific War in 1945. This period can be understood as a progressive nationalist movement, which began as a nationalist revolution and became an ultra-nationalist imperialism (Gordon 2003). These developments were accompanied by powerful ideological movements aimed at building the Japanese identity (Iida 2002). This nationalist revolution had at its core the national polity theory *kokutai* that presented Japan as an extended family derived from the Imperial one, and in which gendered division of labour in the private and public realms was essential (Oguma 2002).

Thus, during this period, the Emperor became Japan's most powerful unifying force, and the idea that Japan was a pure and homogeneous nation was at the centre of the national identity (Suzuki 2005). In order to propagate this ideology among ordinary people, the government relied on various means. First, specific religious and cultural practices and the centralized universal education system were promoted. Between 1870 and 1900, Shinto, combined with Confucian virtues, was considered the national religion and demanded people's obedience to the Emperor and the state (Oguma 2002; Suzuki 2005). Then, according to the Civil Code of 1898, women were strictly confined to the private realm and placed under male authority; they were denied control over assets and decisions like where to live and whom to marry and had to be guided by the ideals of the slogan 'good wife, wise mother' (Uno 1993). The Annual Report of the Minister of Education of the same year indicated that higher education schools for women were designed to instruct females on topics to achieve those ideals (Bacon 2010: 100).

At the beginning of the twentieth century, the proliferation of the press, radio and cinema strongly influenced the Japanese and gender identities in a sociocultural context incorporating the needs of a growing capitalist market where women became central. First, numerous newspapers and magazines were created and written by men and directed at women, giving them advice on how to be better mothers and wives in the new Japan. However, during the 1920s and 1930s, the national industry needed to increase the demand for its consumer goods and required female labour to attend the numerous stores proliferating around cities. Thus, the tone of printed content for women began to change, giving them a curated glimpse of the liberal ideas and fashion trends of women in the United States and Europe and creating new ideals. Nonetheless, it maintained the essence of gender division of labour but in a more attractive way that responded to the industry's developments. Therefore, young single Japanese women in cities acquired new social roles as professional working females – referred to as new women – and they used their money to buy the things they saw in magazines. A few years later, another archetype of young working women was obsessively represented in printed media as an emblem of the consumer and mass culture adopted from the West: the *moga* (modern girl) (Sato 2003). These two representations caused slightly different reactions from the government and ideological leaders of the patriarchal society. The professional new women were seen as a menace to traditional values, but they were an essential factor in achieving national goals; however, the *moga* were perceived as an extreme deviation from tradition and were accused of being just shallow, hedonist, immoral and unpatriotic (Bacon 2010; Sato 2003; Uno 1993).

At the same time, because Japan was immersed in military campaigns, the national sentiment was heavily boosted by the government. All cinema productions were strictly regulated and scrutinized by educators and ideologues to reflect the national ideology that was being pushed at the time (Miyao 2002). Animated films were used to reach young audiences, particularly boys, to romanticize the life and role of soldiers in war (Desser 1995; Nornes and Yukio 2021).

After the Second World War, Allied forces occupied the Japanese territory for nearly a decade. Japan's autonomy and most institutions were respected, but people had to face drastic cultural and social changes in which the Japanese identity was weakened after losing the centrality of the Emperor. Nevertheless, between the 1950s and 1970s, the growing economy and the improvement of the lifestyles of the urban population gave the Japanese elites a new locus for the national identity: society itself. The government and corporations used media to endorse the urban nuclear family as the representation of postwar economic success, and cultural nationalists proudly used the idealized notion of a national middle class as the foundation to promote the idea of homogeneity in Japanese society (Vogel 1971).

Again, this new social ideal was based on the gendered division of labour and produced the male and female archetypes of postwar Japan: the salaryman – white-collar employee or bureaucrat – and the *sengyōshufu* – full-time housewife (Mandujano-Salazar 2017). A typical salaryman had a lifetime job in a stable Japanese company or institution and a salary that grew with seniority and was enough to provide him and his family with a middle-class lifestyle. However, he was expected to be fully dedicated to his organization because that was how he fulfilled his national obligation by supporting the goal of making Japan an economic power (Dasgupta 2010; Hidaka 2010). On the other hand, after graduating from high school, women were expected to contribute to the labour force in auxiliary and non-specialized roles in offices of all kinds of industries, for which they were called 'office ladies' or OL. Although they worked full-time, their contracts were for a specific period and renovated according to the company's needs; these contracts meant that they were not receiving the wages or promotions that men did and could barely sustain themselves. By denying them the same labour conditions that men had, the industry and government pushed women to marry and retire from the workforce to continue fulfilling their social and national duty as *sengyōshufu*, supporting their husbands in the household and nurturing the next generation of Japanese citizens (Yu 2009). Access to financial security was promoted as dependent on young men achieving a salaryman status, directly related to graduating from a prestigious school. Hence, a prosperous future depended on access to high-level education based on the results of merit-based entrance exams. In this process, the role of dedicated mothers became central; they had to keep an eye on their children's education and manage the family budget to get them into extra classes (Gordon 2003). Education and exams were the same for girls and boys, but gender stereotypes predisposed the reasoning behind trying to get into high-level schools: boys studied to get into a top-tier school to secure a good job; girls were expected to get into good schools to meet a promising husband (Tanaka 1995).

Entertainment played a significant role in promoting these new social ideals. In 1953, television was introduced to Japan and changed consumption patterns; television and radio sets became the most desirable commodities that the Japanese industry mass-produced for internal consumption and would later be flag-exporting products. As expected, central for the economic and social aims was the production of attractive television and radio content that promoted imagery evoking the new social success as dependent on the possession of all the appliances and goods produced by the national industry (Ivy 1993; Vogel 1971). Soon, television became the most potent and influential mass medium through animation, fictional dramas, variety and music shows.

There was a consistent and constant portrayal of *sengyōshufu*-centred middle-class households with highly standardized lifestyles, endorsing the discourses about women's responsibility for childrearing and household management and endorsing this as the desirable, bright and prosperous life for women (Lukács 2010; Uno 1993).

However, the notion of culturally homogenized masses involved the transformation into a postmodern society in which the individual got lost in anonymity and was dominated by externally imposed demands. Thus, it is not surprising that at the same time that a considerable majority of Japanese people seemed to align with that national ideal, civil movements and protests peaked, contradicting those images of homogeneous success and happiness. For example, there were social movements against the American army bases in Japan and the interventions of the United States in Vietnam, as well as pro-environmental manifestations and movements in favour of ethnic minorities (Kurokawa 2010; Upham 1993).

In this context, a discourse and cultural nationalist movement centred on the Japanese identity popularized between the 1970s and 1980s with the name of *Nihonron* (theories about Japan), *Nihonjinron* (theories about Japanese people), *Nihon shakairon* (theories about Japanese society) or *Nihon bunkaron* (theories about Japanese culture). The three terms refer to the same ideological movement; in this book, it will be referred to as *Nihonjinron* because it is the most commonly used term in English literature. The *Nihonjinron* revived ideas of other times regarding traditional Japanese values, homogeneity and cultural exceptionality (Befu 2001; Iida 2002; Yoshino 2005). The cultural model promoted followed general ideas recovered from already celebrated ideologists from previous periods, such as Yanagita Kunio and Watsuji Tetsurō, and notions proposed by contemporary Japanese scholars such as Nakane Chie and Doi Takeo, as well as some notable Western scholars studying Japanese society, such as Ruth Benedict, Edwin O. Reischauer and Ezra Vogel (Mandujano 2014a).

Under the premise of national ethnic homogeneity, the authors and promoters of the *Nihonjinron* employed generalizations to define the presumed ethos and characteristic behaviour of Japanese people, which were purportedly also at the core of all institutions. In this regard, the most distinctive feature of the Japanese was said to be their collectivism, as opposed to the individualism favoured in the West. According to this idea, inside the Japanese groups, there is always a hierarchy according to seniority, and everyone recognizes it and acts accordingly (Nakane 1973). This vertical structure is said to be nurtured by paternalistic relations that promote *amae* (an emotional dependence on superiors) strengthening the relationship between them and subordinates (Doi 1981). The background of these types of relations is attributable to the Neo-Confucianism values like filial piety and the notions of *on* (indebtedness), *giri* (obligation) and *sekentei* (decency according to society's standards) (Lebra 2004). Furthermore, it is argued that there is a constant play between the expression of self-consciousness (*honne*) and the expression framed by social conventions (*tatemae*) that makes Japanese people behave in different ways depending on the context they are in and the hierarchies that are at stake without the resultant inconsistency becoming an issue of hypocrisy or dishonesty; these different faces that are used accordingly are the *omote* (the face that is put in accordance to the circumstances) and the *ura* (the truthful mind that is kept from the public) (Doi 1988). The avoidance of conflict and shame, the favouring of harmony and a syncretic inclination were also said to be central to Japanese nature.

Although these ideas originated in Japanese academia, they were rapidly disseminated through media without solid theoretical or methodological support, arguing that those characteristics were the reason behind Japan's reconstruction, economic growth and successful corporative model (Befu 2001). Soon, the Japanese government began endorsing these ideas by publishing and distributing some of the most representative *Nihonjinron* titles and by designing public policies that followed the proposed cultural model, supporting it as a dominant discourse. In this sense, the figure of the *hyōronka* (critic or commentator) in radio, television and press became imperative for the shaping of people's opinions, regardless of most of them not being scholars or scientists. The *nihonjinron* lost its strength as a dominant discourse and cultural movement in the 1990s when Japan faced an economic crisis and many social problems. Nevertheless, the ideas related to the Japanese identity had been assimilated by society so deeply that Befu (2001) suggested that the discourse has achieved the status of civil religion.

The tarento system

After the Second World War, the Japanese celebrity system developed with some peculiarities that influenced the symbolism of media personas, the ways in which audiences make sense of them and the intensity in which people relate to them. In the beginning, the centre of the entertainment industry was the cinema, theatre, radio and print media, which dominated a few stars with specific talents; also, for financial and structural reasons after the war, Japanese media corporations imported much of their cinema, music and television content from the United States. Nonetheless, in the 1960s, when television sets became affordable for most families, media corporations identified the ideological and representational elements that echoed with Japanese audiences and, aligning with the industry's needs to promote national commodities, they began producing content and relegating foreign products (Atkins 2000; Gossmann 2000; Marx 2012).

As in other societies, Japanese stars had an aura of perfection, of being untouchable and living in a different reality than ordinary people; they were meant to be admired but not to be relatable. However, media corporations and the national industry needed to appeal to comprehensive sectors of Japanese consumers and promote the image of the national middle class. Thus, they developed a system relying on television celebrities whose images were symbolically built to appear familiar and relatable to the average individual to become models for audiences to identify with and not feel inferior (Aoyagi 2005; Darling-Wolf 2004; Iwabuchi 2002). Gradually, this system expanded its dominance to all media, absorbing people from very diverse fields and turning them into multifunctional image commodities and all-powerful currencies particular to the Japanese media culture (Lukács 2010). These celebrities are the *tarento* (the Japanese pronunciation of talent, which is used for singular, plural, masculine and feminine) and include the recognizable faces that communicate with Japanese people through daily television and radio shows, theatre, concerts, movies, posters on the trains, billboards on the streets, music listened on the way and labels on the products of the supermarket. This overexposure in the daily life of the Japanese people makes the *tarento* very influential and crucial for propagating ideological discourses.

Galbraith and Karlin (2012) define them as celebrity performers who, using their ability to attract and maintain audiences' attention, are the television discourse's core. Indeed, *tarento* serves as an umbrella category that includes individuals continuously present on television, but they are not limited to it precisely because of their multi functionality. A *tarento* can potentially fill any need of any media production; in fact, they and their management agencies must try to diversify their activities as much as possible because they produce value with their circulation (Lukács 2010). Although in the Japanese media jargon, there is a tendency to use other terms – actor, comedian, idol, model – parallel to the *tarento*, the specificity to call them in one way or another at a particular moment depends on the status of the activity that they are performing in a specific context. Because of this, it is not uncommon to hear the name of the same person referred to sometimes as an idol, then as an actor and others just as a *tarento*. Nonetheless, these distinctions are relevant for regular audiences because the difference in the label used allows them to focus on particular elements of the symbolism that involves that celebrity in the highly intertextual Japanese media context (Mandujano-Salazar 2014).

Therefore, from an analytical point of view, *tarento* is the broadest category embracing many subcategories in the Japanese media landscape: *aidoru* (idol), *joyū/haiyū* (actress/actor), *owarai geinin* (comedian), *kashu* (singer), *anaunsā* (announcer), *kyasutā* (anchor), *moderu* (model), *hyōronka* (critic or 'expert'), *seiyū* (voice actor or actress), *ātisuto* (artist, as in creator) and *senshu* (athlete). Also, it is becoming more common for non-specific celebrities, those who are famous just for being famous, as Boorstin (1992) would say, to become actors, singers or any other genre inside the media. Even if most celebrities have a core activity or ability, those who become popular easily cross genres; also, as media and entertainment develop, more subcategories are included because the system appropriates them to exploit those image commodities to the extreme. This is facilitated by the self-referentiality that characterizes the Japanese media that presents entertainment and tabloid news as socially relevant hard news (Galbraith and Karlin 2012).

Thus, the multifaceted and accelerated circulation of the *tarento* builds 'an intertextual web of meanings that link forms and contents together to produce new meanings' (Galbraith and Karlin 2012: 10). In this context, the audience of Japanese media must draw on a vast cultural knowledge about a *tarento* to fully understand and extract value from a content, a product or a service that is endorsed by that celebrity. In her study about Japanese television during the 1990s, Lukács (2010) found that audiences highly regard this intertextuality because it allows them to join a meta-reality that makes them feel part of a community; they are compelled to expose regularly to the media to acquire the required knowledge about *tarento* and feel included in that meta-reality.

Nevertheless, not all *tarento* have the same presence in media or the ability to get the interest of the audiences or generate in people a positive affective bond; not all *tarento* constitute a significant influence in Japanese society because they do not have the same media power. Because the role of the *tarento* in the Japanese economic system is so essential, the *tarento* power is relevant and acknowledged by companies, media and audiences and has been operationalized into a quarterly ranking that identifies the *tarento* that have the highest level of influence in Japanese society around the year, as well as the core audience of each of them (Talent Power Ranking 2023a). The *tarento* power reflects the power of attraction – the desire of the audiences to see, hear and know more about a *tarento* – and the grade of popularity – how well a *tarento*'s face and name are identified by different sectors of Japanese society.[1] In twentieth-first-century Japan, idols have become the *tarento par excellence*. Although the category has existed since the late 1960s, their symbolic qualities and place in Japanese media have evolved from representing mainly the tastes of teenagers to becoming the centre of the *tarento* system altogether, primarily for their appeal to large audiences (Aoyagi 2005; Karlin 2012; Mandujano-Salazar 2009).

The idols in postwar Japan

More than other *tarento*, idols are symbolic commodities crafted carefully to appeal to up-to-date tastes. Thus, they are the best reflection of the social mood in each period. Social mood is a concept developed from the intersection of sociology, psychology and economics – socionomic theory; it is the aggregate of individual emotional states that influence each other in society and impacts consumer choices (Olson 2006; Ziembinski 2015). Considering this, the logic behind the origin of Japan's idol industry is intimately related to the economic, ideological and social transitions that society faced during the 1960s and 1970s. During that period, the Japanese economy and diverse industries were thriving, and one of their representative products was the television, first in black and white, later in colour. The possession of television in Japanese houses became a symbol of belonging to the national middle class. This was accompanied by the production of diverse content to be watched all day, primarily by housewives, children and teenagers, and the advertising of products and services that the national industry produced, which consolidated Japan's mass consumer society. The market expansion required more identities to be produced and represented by faces to relate them with so the audiences could be interpellated through media audiovisual content. As a result, producer and management companies of idols – commonly known as *jimusho* – flourished and adapted their business models to the new demands of the market in an era of prosperity (Aoyagi 2005; Marx 2012).

In the early 1970s, amid the flourishing *Nihonjinron* discourse, the Japanese music industry, which was expanding, began to differentiate genres: music that expressed the Japanese spirit was called *enka* and interpellated young adult and older generations; in contrast, that inspired by American popular music was called *poppusu* (pop) and had young people as primary market (Yano 2003, 2005). The most prominent example of this transitional period is Misora Hibari, the so-called first Japanese idol, who sang traditional and more contemporary forms of music, reflecting the struggle between traditional Japanese values and the Westernized entertainment elements increasingly popular in postwar society (Shamoon 2009).

At this time, television companies produced their family content to broadcast during weekend afternoons; the music programmes and series in these slots were the settings for the rise of popular idols that appealed to broad audiences. The idol industry flourished within the framework of television audition programmes; the most iconic was *Star Tanjō* (NTV), from where huge names in the Japanese music and entertainment industry started, such as Yamaguchi Momoe and Koizumi Kyoko. The show's format consisted of aspiring singers attending and performing in a contest in which music production companies offered contracts to the winners. This was the origin of the classic idols: they were introduced as average teenagers with big dreams; showed their talent and hard work, and made their debut as singers; performed continuously on music programmes and attracted fans. As their fan base grew, they diversified their activities within the entertainment industry, finally transitioning to worshipped idols in front of and because of the audience (Aoyagi 2005; Sakai 2005). This became a symbolic and practical characteristic of the idols: their success was not related to any exceptional artistic talent – like singers or other performers; it depended entirely on building an affective bond with fans that the industry could exploit.

In the 1980s, amid the bubble economy, with extensive money circulating in society, there was an increasing demand for more idols from a society eager to consume entertainment and to identify with new prosperous and exotic lifestyles. In this context, rock bands known as *visual kei*, like X Japan and Glay, became hugely popular with their androgynous aesthetics and extravagant styles. Idols had considerable competition to conquer a steady base of fans, so the *jimusho's* role became crucial. Like other industries, in music, the producer and management companies began to specialize in producing idols with specific characteristics and images to appeal to new and changing tastes, particularly from young people. The *jimusho* recruited teenagers with a specific potential, crafted their images, promoted them to clients, turned them into idols, coordinated their jobs and supervised them in public and private realms to guarantee that their image among the audience and clients remained coherent. Therefore, the idols' supply proliferated, and their images expanded across content and media. At the same time, the consumption of everything related to them grew; not only their performances and songs or their images in a variety of products were consumed by audiences, but the information and gossip about them also became a profitable product. Numerous periodical idol, fashion and teenager magazines appeared, in which popular idols were the central faces and models. In addition, unique photobooks and calendars focusing on one idol or group were launched by publishing companies and consumed by fans as valuable collectable items.

During the 1990s, the recession caused by the speculative bubble's collapse led to rising unemployment, impacting consumption patterns because people were no longer as inclined to splurge on non-essential products. As a result, the social mood changed, and people felt uncertainty about the future, which made rock and folk music more appealing in the first years of the crisis, and later talented singers. As a result, the idol industry declined relatively; this period is called the idol ice age (*aidoru hyōgaki*). On the other hand, the worldwide fascination for Japanese popular culture at the time meant that the Japanese entertainment industry looked to Asia as a potential market; accordingly, idol management companies aimed to reach foreign audiences and strengthen the place of fan clubs (Aoyagi 2000).

By the turn of the twenty-first century, due to the strategies of two influential *jimusho* leaders – Johnny Kitagawa and Akimoto Yasushi – male and female idols reached a central place in the Japanese entertainment industry, leading the music market and being part of most media productions. All-female idol groups, like AKB48 and all its sister groups, are very successful and follow the model created by Akimoto, enjoying success in Japan and other parts of East Asia (Galbraith 2012). This model focuses on the female-only group's concept – idols that fans can meet – and the numerous members constantly changing according to fans' demands. The idols' ages go from teenagers to women in their twenties, and they constantly perform in events where fans – mostly male – can get close to them and shake their hands in exchange for some type of consumption. Although this model has proved to be very successful and is representative of contemporary Japanese media culture, the continuous change of the girls makes it difficult for the general Japanese audience to grasp the essence of their personalities and images.

Nonetheless, they still embody relevant ideas about Japanese women. The media narratives regarding AKB48 and similar groups motivate the idealization of a sexualized childlike female image. These idols are images of production and consumption, symbolically oscillating 'between an unreachable ideal (the pure) and infinitely available material (the sexual)' (Galbraith 2012: 199). They are represented as an ideal archetype of doll-like, petite girls whose success and position in the group are undeniably related to their ability to appeal to male fans and the male producer. The fact that they are exchangeable members in their groups denotes the low value of these idols as individual personalities. Also, the retirement of members when they are getting into their late twenties reinforces the hegemonic femininity discourse: a woman is desired in the public sphere when she is young and has a high sex appeal, but when she matures her worth is found in the private roles of wife and mother (Mandujano-Salazar 2014). Thus, this female idol model reinforces the traditional ideas of the Japanese patriarchal society.

On the other hand, there is the idol model developed by Johnny's Jimusho, a company that specializes in producing all-male groups. In contrast to the female idols mentioned before, Johnny's model relies on crafting and nurturing the individual personalities of each member, giving them considerable longevity in media. This company's model and its idols' social and ideological roles will be the focus of the rest of the book.

The rise of Johnny's Jimusho

Johnny's Jimusho is, perhaps, the most recognized idol production company in Japan. Japanese people, regardless of whether they are fans or not, are generally aware of the company's existence and the public image of its idols. This awareness has to do with the company's historical development since the 1960s. However, the creator behind it, known as Johnny Kitagawa – generally referred to by media and idols as Johnny-san – remained mostly reserved for decades, giving only a few interviews; most of what is known about him is from anecdotes told by the idols he produced. There are not many photographs of him, something peculiar for one of the most powerful men in the Japanese entertainment industry.

In 1931, Johnny was born in the United States in a *nikkei* family, a family of Japanese emigrants. He was the youngest of three siblings, and his father, Kitagawa Taido, was a Buddhist priest in Los Angeles. The family returned to Japan in 1933; thus, he spent his childhood in Japan. However, the Kitagawa siblings went to Los Angeles to continue their studies when the Second World War ended, while their father stayed in Japan to manage one of the professional baseball teams. In 1950, Johnny took his first steps into entertainment production when he had the opportunity to work as a stage manager for Misora Hibari's concert in Los Angeles (Sansupo 2019). Nonetheless, during the 1950s, as part of the American army, he had to move between the United States, Japan and Korea. His post in this country gave him a chance to interact with orphan children, which he enjoyed, according to one of the few interviews he gave during his lifetime; he also declared that he had always wanted to be involved in show business on the production side (Ui 2019).

Consequently, at the beginning of the 1960s, while living in Tokyo and working in the office of information for the United States embassy, he followed his father's example and used his days off to coach a children's baseball team, which he eventually called 'Johnny's boys' (Shūkan Josei PRIME 2019). Two years later, he established the company Johnny's Jimusho and selected four boys from the baseball team – Iino Osami, Maie Hiromi, Aoi Teruhiko and Nakatani Ryo – to turn them into an idol group named 'Johnny's'. The group released its first single, *Wakai namida,* in 1964, considered their official debut; the following year, they appeared in the *Kōhaku Uta Gassen*[2] and released numerous hit songs until 1967, when they disbanded (Yano 2016). The group was a major success; their songs and the members appeared in television series, motion pictures, musicals and plays.

In 1968, Johnny's Jimusho debuted its second group – Four Leaves – with Kita Koji, Aoyama Takashi, Egi Toshi and Orimo Masao; this group had formed the previous year to perform as a back dancer for Johnny's (Nikkan Sports 2019b). Four Leaves is considered the first all-male idol group that sang and danced. At this time, Johnny's older sister, Mary, joined the company; their goal was to create idol groups in which all members were considered stars, contrary to other popular groups of the time that had one popular member and the rest were merely supporters (Yano 2016). Accordingly, Four Leaves as a group and all the members individually participated recurrently in variety shows, television series, movies, radio programmes, musicals, plays and commercials. During the decade it was active, the group released more than thirty singles and participated for seven recurrent years in the *Kōhaku Uta Gassen* (NHK).

In the meantime, Johnny's Jimusho recruited more boys who were prepared to dance and sing while acting as back dancers for Four Leaves. In 1970, from those boys, the four-member group Juke Box debuted with the single *Sayonara no Inori;* and, in 1972, Go Hiromi debuted with the single *Otoko no ko onna no ko,* and soon became one of the most popular idols of the time (Nikkan Sports 2019b).

At the beginning of 1975, the Kitagawa siblings turned the company into a joint-stock corporation officially registered as Johnny & Associates, but remaining as the only shareholders. In the next decade, Johnny's Jimusho continued producing male idols and began to apply another strategy to popularize them and release musical productions as soloists and in small groups: the collaboration with television series productions in which some of the idols were main actors and could also sing some of the series' theme songs. This strategy was behind the most representative names and groups of the decade. In the first generation, Kondo Masahiko, Tahara Toshihiko and Nomura Yoshio formed the so-called Tanokin Trio due to their popularity and acting in the school series *3-nen B-gumi Kinpachi Sensei* (TBS). Another generation was formed by Fukawa Toshikazu, Motoki Masahiro and Yakumaru Hirohide, who formed the group Shibukigakitai, which resulted from their participation in the school series *2-nen B-gumi Senpachi Sensei* (TBS).

The other debuted groups followed the previous strategy of being formed from the back dancers of the senior groups. Shōnentai, formed by Higashiyama Noriyuki, Uekusa Katsuhide and Nishikiori Kazukiyo, acquired great popularity before its official debut in 1985, already participating in musical shows, concerts and winning awards as a unit (Nikkan Sports 2019b). Even today, some of these idols in their fifties continue to be managed by the company and have become renowned actors and producers.

By the end of the 1980s, Johnny's Jimusho began experimenting with larger groups and other types of images and music. In 1987, Hikaru GENJI, a group of seven members performing on roller skates, debuted and remained active until 1995. Then, in 1988, the company debuted its first rock band, Otokogumi, formed by four members (Nikkan Sports 2019b; Yano 2016). The company's name became a brand identified by society and, amid the idol boom of the 1980s, the company received numerous requests from boys – or their family members – to join. In this way, Johnny's Jimusho was able to effectively develop the junior system – an apprentice category – which would become crucial within the industry during the following years. At the time, some young women were among the back dancers, but the company decided to specialize in developing the male idol industry.

Johnny Kitagawa was directly involved in the selection of aspiring teenagers through a peculiar practice of observing the collective auditions without saying who he was. Instead, he handed out drinks or food and talked informally with the boys; in a few cases, he scouted boys and invited them to join without an audition (Ui 2019). By this time, the Kitagawa siblings had established a clear style for their idols, and Johnny could identify how boys' faces and bodies would mature to fit what came to be known as Johnny's type: pretty boys who could play with androgyny for the pleasure of female fans (Darling-Wolf 2004; McLellan 2008).

However, the physical image was only one element in these idols; more important was that their behaviour within the industry reflected Japanese values. Kitagawa created a structure that followed the principle of a traditional Japanese household (*ie*). Seniority and filial piety were greatly respected, so older and more experienced boys guided the younger ones; but, at the same time, to promote unity among them, once a boy entered the company as a trainee – or junior – he could refer to the rest, regardless of seniority, with the suffix *kun,* which is added to names of those peers who are of the same lower hierarchy than oneself (Mandujano 2014a; Mandujano-Salazar 2014a).

By the 1990s, most groups and solo artists launched in the previous decade disbanded or scaled down their activities, something that was expected because, at that time, an idol was considered to be intrinsically related to youth. Nonetheless, the idols that debuted in that decade eventually challenged this idea, expanding the career of male idols and turning Johnny's Jimusho into *the* producer of male idols in Japan. On this aim, first, the company consolidated the media activities of the junior base, creating popular idols even before their official debut. Such is the case of Takizawa Hideaki, the leader of Johnny's junior during the second half of the 1990s, who became famous among general audiences, starring in popular television series and hosting variety shows before debuting. The company also began to promote the participation of the idols in the creative process behind their activities, from writing and composing some of their songs to being in charge of the design of their stage clothes and concerts. In this way, these idols evolved, and the entertainment industry recognized them as more than teenage idols who sold their images to a small audience; instead, as they matured and moved into more serious media activities, they expanded their fan base and were able to continue as idol groups regardless of being well into their thirties and forties.

However, not everything was running smoothly for the company. In 1999, a report from *Shūkan Bunshun,* one of the weekly investigative magazines not aligned with mainstream media, printed a series of interviews with some ex-juniors who alleged that Johnny Kitagawa had sexually molested them when they were teenagers and part of the trainee idols (Bunshun Online 2023; Cyzo Woman Henshubu 2023; Joho Station Tokuneta 2019; Nakamura 2022). Nonetheless, formal accusations were never made and mainstream media did not cover the situation. In fact, Kitagawa sued the magazine for defamation

Table 1 Johnny's Jimusho idols debuted between 1962 and 2022.

Name of the idol or group	Year of debut	Number of members at the debut	Year of disbandment or retirement from the company	Name	Year of debut	Number of members at the debut	Year of disbandment or retirement from the company
Johnny's	1964	4	1967	NEWS	2003	9	
Four leaves	1968	4	1978	Kanjani ∞	2004	8	
Juke Box	1970	4	1973	KAT-TUN	2006	6	
Go Hiromi	1971	1	1975	Yamashita Tomohisa	2006	1	2020
Tanokin Trio	1979	3	1983	Tegomasu (temporary)	2006	2	2020
Shibugakitai	1982	3	1988	Hey! Say! JUMP	2007	10	
Shōnentai	1985	3	2020	NYC (temporary)	2010	3	2013
Hikaru GENJI	1987	7	1995	Kis-My-Ft2	2011	7	
Otokogumi	1988	4	1993	Sexy Zone	2011	5	
SMAP	1991	6	2016	A.B.C-Z	2012	5	
TOKIO	1994	5	2021	Johnny's WEST	2014	7	
V6	1996	6	2021	King & Prince	2018	5	

Name of the idol or group	Year of debut	Number of members at the debut	Year of disbandment or retirement from the company
Kinki Kids	1997	2	
Arashi	1999	5	In a hiatus since 2021
Tackey & Tsubasa	2002	2	2018

Name	Year of debut	Number of members at the debut	Year of disbandment or retirement from the company
SixTONES	2020	6	
Snow Man	2020	9	
Naniwa Danshi	2021	7	
Travis Japan	2022	7	

Source: Elaborated by the author.

and won, so these allegations remained a rumour acknowledged by most fans and the Japanese society, but they did not affect the relevance of the company, the popularity of the idols or the demand of hundreds of children and teenagers to enter the junior base in the hope of becoming famous.

From 2000 to 2019, more than a dozen groups debuted, with close supervision from Kitagawa. After that, however, he left most of the company's responsibility to Mary, her daughter – Fujishima Julie Keiko – and Iijima Michi, the manager who successfully turned one of the groups – SMAP – into the first 'national idols' (Nikkan Sports 2019b). After Johnny's death in the summer of 2019, Fujishima became the corporation's president; since then and until the beginning of 2023, another four groups debuted. Table 1 shows the idols – solo and groups – that Johnny's Jimusho has produced in six decades.

The male-idol factory: Strategies behind the production of Johnny's idols in the twenty-first century

In Japan, after the overindulgence of the 1980s, the 1990s were a decade in which a disenchanted mood took place. The economy contracted, but Japan's music market continued to be the second largest in the world – behind only the United States – considering revenues from the sale of music and music videos both digitally and in any physical format (CD, DVD, Blue-Ray, cassette, minidisc, LP, VHS and the like) and licenses for reproduction by third parties (radio, television, restaurants, bars and so forth) (IFPI 2022; Pastukhov 2022; Recording Industry Association of Japan 2022). This was mainly owing to the singer-songwriters, who expressed the social mood in a way that felt more authentic, rarely appeared in the media if it was not to promote their songs, and appealed to large portions of the population, regardless of gender and age. On the other hand, the idols' market niche was too small and specific. In the case of Johnny's idols, their music was primarily consumed by teenage female fans with little disposable income. Then, at the turn of the century, the Japanese music industry suffered a contraction due to the prolonged recession, technological changes and demographic trends (Recording Industry Association of Japan 2000).

Nevertheless, in 2010, Japan even surpassed the United States in terms of retail value, despite having less than half the population of its counterpart; this time, Johnny's idols dominated the annual charts (Recording Industry Association of Japan 2011, 2012). One strategy that Johnny's Jimusho had been applying for a decade was the rapid production of idol groups. Another was the idols' incursion into media roles that were previously unthinkable for this type of *tarento*, which increased their general appeal and longevity in the industry. That year, eleven groups were active, involving fifty-five idols between the ages of fourteen and forty; this meant that Johnny's Jimusho no longer depended only on teenagers as consumers but also on adult women who followed the older groups. Furthermore, of those idols, 64 per cent wrote lyrics for their groups' songs, 44 per cent composed music and 56 per cent played musical instruments, making them appear more authentic and talented for broader music consumer sectors (Mandujano-Salazar 2009). In this context, Johnny's Jimusho also launched its recording labels to produce the music of its idols and applied strategies to increase its fan base. These strategies, along with those of female idol producers like Akimoto Yasushi, successfully repositioned idols in the Japanese music industry by promoting the consumption of thousands of singles, albums and music videos, which boosted the music industry as a whole.[1]

This chapter builds on basic market theory and cultural and media studies concepts to present the stages of the production model that Johnny's Jimusho developed for its idols, which resulted in the company's domination of the Japanese entertainment industry in the twenty-first century. The methodology followed, first, a documentary and statistical analysis of sources from the Recording Industry Association of Japan (2000, 2001, 2004, 2006, 2007, 2008, 2009, 2010, 2011, 2012, 2022), Oricon rankings (Oricon ME Inc n.d.), Talent Power Ranking (2023a), Johnny's Jimusho Official Website (Johnny & Associates 2023a) and fan-club releases, which allowed to identify the evolution of idols in the Japanese market and select the most representative case for study. The second stage was an interpretative textual analysis of that selected case's media productions between 1999 and 2010, participant observation and interviews with Japanese fans, by which the process for a group to become famous and develop a stable and broad fan base was deconstructed. This chapter presents the general context of Johnny's in the music industry during the 2000s to select the most representative case, then examines the production cycle of a group (or unit) in three stages: recruitment and formation in the Junior base, debut, and diversification and expansion.

The group representing the male-idol model of the twenty-first century

Aoyagi (2005: 3) said that 'idols are planned to contribute to the establishment of the industry in the market by virtue of their abilities to attract people and act as role models'. Accordingly, Johnny's Jimusho targets two types of consumers: the audience that consumes the music products and the idols as symbolic commodities through the products with their image, and the media and other industries companies that hire the idol to exploit his image, name or skills for various purposes related to those companies' main products. Despite this, the type of consumer that determines to a greater extent the development and promotion strategies is the niche of the audience to which the idols aim to appeal and interpellate. If Johnny's Jimusho succeeds in this endeavour, it will be easier and more profitable to negotiate with the other large block of clients, the industries.

As in any market, the producer relies on the expectations of potential consumers – audience and companies – to create a desirable product that can bring economic benefits. On the other hand, consumers are not passive; they influence production by deciding whether or not to consume what is being offered. It is relevant to understand that although Johnny's Jimusho has created a male-idol market that is basically a monopoly in Japan, domestic consumers can enter and exit from that market freely due to the wide variety of substitute products they have access to, like dozens of Japanese *tarento* and hundreds of foreign artists and celebrities. If they consume within this specific market, it is because the products offered by the company satisfy their preferences or interpellate them. However, the company must implement strategies to maintain the status quo, especially when direct competition appears – that is, the entrance into the Japanese market, in 2005, of Korean male idols. In this way, the tastes, preferences and ideas of all the agents involved in the market are reflected in the symbolic and discursive characteristics of the successful idols of an epoch. Therefore, by studying the development of Johnny's most successful products and analysing the actions carried out by the supply side, it is also possible to infer the characteristics that consumers, especially the first group – the general audience – value in the products offered. These qualities are relevant because they reflect the social and cultural values prevailing in the market.

It is convenient to select a representative case to examine the strategies of Johnny's Jimusho, although the information available from all the company idols will enrich the analysis, predominantly for the first stage. In Japanese entertainment, some key indicators to measure an idol group's activity and success are the release of musical singles and albums. These are crucial not only for the direct economic value but also because they involve multiple promotional activities, and they produce more information that enhances the intertextuality that builds the identities and values represented by each group, reinforcing their social impact. Analysing Johnny's groups with more and most successful musical productions during the first decade of the century, it was found that besides holding concerts at the largest venues in Japan – the Tokyo, Nagoya, Sapporo, Kyocera and Fukuoka Domes – they had increased activity on other media and entertainment activities, such as participation in films, television series, theatre plays and numerous commercials.

In 2006, Johnny's Jimusho stood out at the top of the Japanese music market for the first time, becoming the leader in singles sales with the debut of KAT-TUN and productions from its nine active idol units that year (Recording Industry Association of Japan 2007). Before that, some of the singles released by the company's groups – like SMAP, Kinki Kids or Arashi – had entered the annual top-ten sales charts; however, it was from then on that productions by Johnny's groups began to occupy around a quarter of the total number of places in the list of the 100 best-selling singles in Japan (Oricon ME Inc n.d.). Likewise, the presence of Johnny's Jimusho idols or productions released by them in the various categories of awards granted by the Recording Industry Association of Japan increased significantly; for example, Best Music Video, Best Albums, Best Singles and Artists of the Year. This last award is the most prestigious in the music industry because it represents the artist with the highest sales of the year, including all types of productions related to music.

Table 2 shows the active groups in 2010, the number of singles and albums they released from 1999 to 2010, and the share of these related to the total of Johnny's Jimusho single and album productions. Based on these, Arashi was the top performer in both categories. Also, between 2008 and 2010, in the context of the growing popularity of Korean idols in Japan, Arashi had

Table 2 Johnny's Jimusho idols' musical productions, 1999–2010.

Name	Year of debut	Number of members in 2010	Number of singles released from 1999 to 2010	Share among Johnny's	Number of albums released from 1999 to 2010	Share among Johnny's
SMAP	1991	5	13	7%	10	14%
TOKIO	1994	5	27	14%	8	11%
V6	1996	6	28	14%	10	14%
Kinki Kids	1997	2	24	12%	12	16%
Arashi	1999	5	34	18%	14	19%
Tackey & Tsubasa	2002	2	11	6%	3	4%
NEWS	2003	6	14	7%	4	5%
Kanjani ∞	2004	7	15	8%	5	7%
KAT-TUN	2006	5	13	7%	5	7%
Yamashita Tomohisa	2006	1	3	2%	0	0%
Tegomasu (temporary unit)	2006	2	5	3%	1	1%
Hey! Say! JUMP	2007	10	6	3%	1	1%
NYC (temporary unit)	2010	3	1	1%	0	0%

Source: Elaborated by the author.

top-selling products in various categories and won Artist of the Year in 2010, a first for Johnny's Jimusho. Therefore, it was chosen as the case of analysis for the production cycle of male idols in Japan. Arashi – that means storm – is a five-member group that made its official debut in 1999 and went into a hiatus at the end of 2020 after more than a decade of dominating the Japanese entertainment industry. The members are Ohno Satoshi, Sakurai Sho, Aiba Masaki, Ninomiya Kazunari and Matsumoto Jun, and they entered the trainee base of Johnny's junior between 1994 and 1996.

The junior base

Developing a new idol unit at Johnny's Jimusho begins with recruiting prospects in the junior base. This stage fulfils three purposes for the company. First, the juniors support the shows and other works of the debuted idols, acting primarily as back dancers. Second, through these activities and others designed for their artistic preparation, the management can identify those with the most significant potential to succeed. Finally, the juniors become a product on their own; through their training activities and the support of other units, fans get to know them and begin choosing their favourites, so the company can sell their images and select the ones to launch officially.

During this stage, the target consumers are women under the age of twenty. However, this does not mean that consumers with other characteristics are left outside the market. On the contrary, there is a strong dependence on men under eighteen and adult women as fans for nurturing the junior base; although they are usually regular consumers of other products of the company, this is, they are fans of debuted idols. Analysing the interviews with Johnny's idols in magazines, radio and television programmes, it was found that there are three patterns by which the aspiring idols apply to the company. The sample included the thirty-six idols who debuted between 1999 and 2010; twenty-one joined the company between 1994 and 1998, and the other fifteen from 1999 to 2006.

The first pattern for deciding to enter Johnny's Jimusho is the applicant's interest in becoming an idol due to admiration for one of the already popular idols or for liking to dance and wanting to be with other boys who like the same. This circumstance is linked, in most cases, to the initial influence of their mothers or sisters who are fans of some Johnny's idol and take them to concerts and live performances. Another reason for young boys to develop an interest in joining the company is the popularity of idols among schoolmates. In these situations, admiration and empathy are mixed in the aspirants, who begin to identify with a particular idol, usually, the one preferred by the women around them (mother, sisters, cousins or classmates). They admire the idol's ability to attract people and begin to consider the possibility of becoming idols themselves. The second pattern concerns a mother's interest in her son joining the company due to her admiration for the idols and the desire for her child to become one. Finally, the third pattern is that of female fans of Johnny's idols who, trying to get close to them, convince a young brother, cousin or male friend to apply to join the company. In the last two cases, female acquaintances sometimes send the applications without telling the boys, and they know about it until they receive a call or letter from the company telling them to go to an audition.

The data in Table 3 show significant changes in the characteristics of entry into the junior base between idols who joined before and after 1999. The first has to do with a decrease in the average age of enrolment, which went down from thirteen to eleven years and seven months. This means that idols who joined before 1999 were secondary schoolers, while those who joined after

Table 3 Patterns of enrolment of idols debuted between 1999 and 2010.

	Idols debuted between 1999 and 2010	Idols who joined between 1994 and 1998	Idols who joined from 1999 to 2006
Average age of enrolment	12.5 years old	13 years old	11.6 years old
Reason 1: He wanted to join	66%	47.60%	93%
Reason 2: His mother wanted him to join	17%	28.60%	0%
Reason 3: His sister, friend or other female acquaintance wanted him to join	17%	23.80%	7%

Source: Elaborated by the author.

1999 were still in elementary school when they entered the junior base. This change is related to the second one, which is the significant increase in the number of idols who decided to enrol by themselves. The main reason for these changes is the expansion of the market during the first decade of the century, as part of the strategies aimed at opening new market sectors and reinforcing the traditional ones, as will be discussed in detail in the following sections. This development reflects the fact that Johnny's idols' symbolism and narratives no longer appeal only to female audiences; they are reaching male children and teenagers, so the need for intermediation on the part of female fans was eliminated.

Once the applicants enter the junior base, the production process begins based on the creation of role models. As Aoyagi (2005: 10) said about the Japanese idol phenomenon in general: 'The idol industry develops socialization rituals that provide, to Japanese teenagers, a path that links the person with society according to what the producers perceive as appropriate personal appearances and qualities.' At Johnny's Jimusho, the junior stage is a crucial element for the formation of the personality, popularity and artistic potential of idol trainees.

The producer relies on two principal activities to support this process: one related to their function as support for debuted idols, and the other related to their position as a product on its own. The first involves dancing and, sometimes, singing in concerts, plays, musicals and media presentations of the debuted groups. On these occasions, the juniors have a secondary role, but when a junior unit or one of the trainees stands out for quality or popularity, they gain more space and time. These activities, in which they are not the centre of attention, allow the juniors to get comfortable on stage while they develop the artistic and technical abilities needed as Johnny's idol. They also understand the importance placed by the company on respecting hierarchies inside Johnny's structure and in media in general, which is an essential symbolic element of role models.

The second type of activities involves starring in musical and variety programmes, acting in dramas, films, musicals and plays, and performing in concerts specific to this category. These are the activities and promotions followed also for debuted idols, with the difference of the notorious increase in the amount and variety of works and their prominence in media. The similarity has to do with the fact that the junior category becomes a product that helps create a fan base for the next generation of debuted idols. During the period analysed, it is estimated that approximately 300 boys were part of the regular junior base, from which only about 10 per cent were part of junior units, often receiving their own columns in television shows and idol magazines, as well as greater participation as support of the debuted groups, which meant higher possibilities of debuting. This significant exposure in media depends on the junior's aptitude in one of the priority areas of the idol's activities – singing, dancing, acting and modelling – but also on his ability to show his personality in the chances he has and obtain a positive reaction from the audience. These elements develop simultaneously during the junior-dedicated television shows and through columns in the monthly idol magazines in which the company presents the idols' updated information.

The regular television shows function as a stage for juniors to demonstrate their artistic skills, predominantly in dancing and singing, but they also allow the trainees to develop their personalities in front of the public and form bonds with fans. This situation is clear when analysing the time distribution in the most relevant juniors' show, *The Shōnen Club*. The show has been broadcast weekly, since 2000, by Japan's public broadcaster Nippon Hōsō Kyōkai (NHK), which indicates the symbiosis between mainstream media and Johnny's Jimusho (NHK n.d.a). In a sample of ten random episodes – one of each year between 2000 and 2010 – about twenty-two minutes of the average of forty-two minutes of running time (excluding commercials) were dedicated to musical acts and the rest to segments where juniors expressed themselves in other ways, like talking about their daily lives or their ideas and opinions on a variety of topics. However, juniors also participate in variety shows aimed at families. In Japan, there is one public broadcaster, the NHK, and four national-reaching private ones: Fuji Television (Fuji TV), Nippon Television (NTV), Asahi Television (Asahi TV) and Tokyo Broadcasting System (TBS). Thus, Johnny's Jimusho arranges for the juniors to have programmes across broadcasters. In the analysed period, the most representative juniors' regular television shows were *Ai Love Junior* (TV Tokyo), *Music Jump* (NHK), *8-ji da J* (TV Asahi), *Gakibara Teigoku 2000!* (TBS), *USO?! Japan* (TBS), *Hadaka no Shōnen* (TV Asahi), *YOU-tachi* (NTV) and *Hyakushikiō* (Fuji TV). All these were broadcast for one year or longer between 1996 and 2010.

On the other hand, idol magazines repeatedly present the general personal data of juniors like their full name, date of birth, blood type, Johnny's idol they admire, the reason for joining the company, hobbies and favourite food. Also, the magazines print the juniors' essays on various topics unrelated to their work but their personal life, their preferences regarding women, and their expectations for their future as adults. Furthermore, the media constantly monitors fans' opinions and the juniors' popularity through different means. One is by publicly presenting the letters and postcards that fans send to the juniors' fan club or directly to the shows or magazines, showing trends on the juniors who receive more messages. Another common way is through seemingly irrelevant surveys; for example, asking fans for their favourite juniors, the one they would like to have as a boyfriend, or the one that dances better. These surveys have valuable functions: first, to give the trainees feedback for improvement; second, to allow Johnny's Jimusho to identify the juniors with a solid fan base that may be ready to debut; third, to let fans know how their favourite idols are doing, so they can show more support to see them debut; finally, to give media and other companies information about the potential value of juniors for endorsing their products.

Each aspirant's duration in this stage differs and officially ends when he debuts solo or as part of a group. Nonetheless, the juniors who make their debut are only a few. At least until September 2023 – when writing this book – the company did not have a rule about how long juniors had to be part of the trainee base in order to debut. Therefore, the renovation was an organic process; the juniors who were not fit for the job, did not achieve popularity among fans or were getting older without a possibility of making their debut, left the company. However, since spring 2023, Johnny's Jimusho established twenty-two as the maximum age for juniors; those who do not debut must leave the company (Shūkan Josei PRIME 2023a). Consequently, the junior base is constantly nurtured by new members who are attracted by the debuted idols and, through the training, Johnny's Jimusho selects those with the better potential to succeed and commercializes the process. Thus, when the company launches a new idol to the market, it already has a consumer base – the fans – ready to receive the new product. Furthermore, because fans were part of the maturation process of the new idols, they are aware of their personalities and what they represent and obtain a high utility from consumption, remaining loyal throughout the years.

Debut and development of image

The second stage in the strategies of Johnny's Jimusho consists of the debut of idol units. If the junior base is a unit with variable membership and regular activities, a debuted group indicates stability in members and continuously changing and expanding activities. With the debuted groups, the company expands the market and its entire business through specific strategies. During the analysis period – 1999 to 2010 – three permanent groups debuted with a single to be used as the theme song for the Volleyball World Cup or Grand Prix: Arashi, NEWS and Hey! Say! JUMP. In these cases, the company formed the groups less than three months before the debut of popular juniors who were not already a unit. Hence, the groups were presented to the audience as original products and had to work to build a group identity to attract more fans than those they had individually. In contrast, the other three units that debuted during that time were junior units with more than two years of working together and with a fan base that pushed for their debut through surveys and fan letters. Regardless of the history behind their debut, groups must develop their image, separating themselves from that of juniors. To achieve this, the company uses three strategies: constantly releasing music singles, regular columns and covers in idol magazines and holding massive concerts. Although these strategies are used throughout the unit's active life, they are crucial at the beginning to create a stable consumer base wider than teenage fans.

After the exhaustive analysis of materials, it is evident that the core of these is the release of musical productions, mainly in the form of physical singles. In fact, the dominant pattern that marks the debut of an idol group in Johnny's Jimusho is the release of a single. This becomes particularly important because they contain the presentation of the groups. There is a difference in the contents of the lyrics of the debut songs for the newly formed groups and those with a history in the junior stage. Because they already have a fan base, the latter did not require a presentation through their musical productions. Meanwhile, the groups formed a few weeks before their debut had to get recognition as a unit from the general public and the media. To achieve this, both the title of the single and the song's lyrics refer to the new group and the meaning of its name. For example, Arashi's debut single was called *A.Ra.Shi*, and the lyrics repeated the name; the same with NEWS' single *NEWS Nippon*, and Hey! Say! JUMP's *Ultra Music Power*, which repeated the meaning of the units' names.

Then, in their first year of activities, the groups in the sample released an average of 2.5 singles and 2.3 annually after that (see Table 4). For Johnny's Jimusho, the continuous release of singles is a strategy for placing and strengthening idol units in the market. The singles' importance is that they allow the groups to carry out frequent publicity activities that positively impact their recognition among the general audience, potentially expanding the consumer sector while consolidating the original fan base. The release of a single also involves making promotional videos – commonly referred to as PVs – that music channels, music stores, streaming sites and other media broadcast incessantly. The images of the PVs are also used for television spots and print advertising, promoting the single and the recognition of the groups' members because their faces are the focus in most takes for those initial videos.

One strategy of Johnny's Jimusho to sell more copies of a single is releasing at least two – sometimes even four – different versions only available in physical format. These contain diverse coupling songs, karaoke versions of the main song, adjunct DVDs with the PVs or the making of the PVs, or special booklets. All these elements are highly valuable materials for fans, so they are motivated to buy all versions. Additionally, to promote their singles, the groups appear on numerous music and variety television shows where, in addition to

Table 4 Singles released by units debuted from 1999 to 2010.

Group	Singles released during the first twelve months	Singles released from the second year to 2010	Promotional Videos (PVs) from debut to 2010	Active years from debut to 2010	Average singles from the second year to 2010
Arashi	3	31	39	11	3.1
Tackey & Tsubasa	1	10	15	8	1.4
NEWS	3	11	14	7	1.8
Kanjani ∞	2	13	15	6	2.6
KAT-TUN	3	10	14	4	3.3
Hey! Say! JUMP	3	3	6	3	1.5
Average	2.5	No relevant	No relevant	No relevant	2.3

Source: Elaborated by the author.

performing, they talk about their lives or the other works to which the single relates – like a television series or movie in which a member participates. However, they rarely talk about the meaning of the lyrics or the artistic development of the musical composition, in part because they are not usually involved in that part of the production but mainly because the talk section of those shows aims to give audiences a glimpse of the idols' personalities. The same pattern can be recognized in music, fashion and entertainment magazines, where they occupy numerous columns for promotion, in addition to being on the covers and getting more pages in idol magazines, as will be detailed later. Although participation in these media is carried out not only for the promotion of singles but also for the release of albums, concerts and tours, and other special events, the frequency of the production of singles compared to albums or concerts is three times higher.

In contrast, the other key strategies in this stage aim to strengthen the original consumer sector: fans. These include establishing an official fan club, appearing in regular columns in idol magazines and holding concert tours. As soon as a new unit debuts, Johnny's Jimusho establishes a fan club in which anyone with a Japanese address can enrol after paying the enrolment fee and annual membership, a total of 5,000 yen the first year and 4,000 yen after. The fans who are members receive a monthly newsletter, an annual personalized birthday card and gift, access to content and exhibitions available only to the fan club, and the chance to obtain concert tickets – although that is not guaranteed, particularly for the most popular shows (Johnny & Associates 2023a).

Concerts are the strategy used by the company to consolidate the most loyal sector of consumers of each unit and, at the same time, to promote the junior base. During the first year of a group's debut, several events are held at least in some of the largest cities in Japan – Tokyo, Yokohama, Osaka, Nagoya, Sapporo or Fukuoka. The primary purpose of concerts is to promote the relationship between the unit and the most dedicated fans because tickets are available only through the official fan club. Once the company announces the dates and venues of a group's tour, the members of the fan club receive a template in which they can request a maximum of four tickets for the events they wish to attend; they must also indicate their preference. The main characteristics of Johnny's concerts are that applying for a ticket does not guarantee getting it and that all tickets for a tour have the same cost. The company selects the fans' applications and the events they can get tickets for through a lottery system according to demand, loyalty as a fan club member, and some other factors that Johnny's Jimusho does not publicly explain. The selected fans get a notification, and when they complete the purchase, the company randomly assigns their seats. This system allows the company to have a high level of control over concert attendees, which results in better organization and safety for both the audience and the idols.[2] Furthermore, it creates a sense of exclusivity and fortune that increases the value of the concerts for fans, who perceive a greater utility in attending after enduring the process, and it also boosts fans' interest in joining the fan club and paying the fee. On the other hand, because all attendees pay the same amount for their tickets, regardless of their seats, the company and the idols spend considerable time and resources to design a show in which fans feel close to the idols. On this aim, throughout the years, the company has developed some devices that allow the idols to move around the venues and reach various levels of the stage. Some of these have been ideas of idols that proved valuable enough to be used in concerts of all the groups, for example, mobile platforms and distribution of corridors that surround and cross the areas of the audience.

A typical concert has an average duration of two hours and forty-five minutes in which, uninterruptedly, at least one of the members is in front of the audience. Throughout the show, there are many changes of costumes and two or three long blocks of performances combined with a few minutes of casual conversation among the group members, which also encourages interaction between them and the audience. In addition, the choreographies and the movement of the idols on stage are prepared to make optimal use of the space, distributing the time spent around each venue sector so that all fans get a clear and close view of each member. Thus, concerts reinforce the base of loyal consumers, who feel rewarded by having access to limited products and opportunities. Also, television variety shows and other media promote images and short videos of the concerts, boosting the group's recognition among the general audience. These strategies consolidate a consumer sector for the debuted groups and remain pillars of marketing throughout their career.

On the other hand, the monthly idol magazines that target teenage girls are essential for the regular promotion of the idols because they focus on presenting photographs and interviews with Johnny's Jimusho's units. The magazines following the Johnny's idols for decades are *Myojo, Potato, Poporo, Wink up* and *duet*. Four of these ostentatiously let such goals be seen in phrases attached to their titles: 'Super Idol Magazine' (*duet*), 'The magazine created by you and the stars' (*Potato*), 'Hyper visual magazine for girls' (*Wink up*) and 'Interview content magazine for ladies' (*Poporo*). The idol magazines dedicate regular sections to each debuted unit and juniors, each containing a group photograph and then some in which one or two members occupy each page. They also present the interviews in which the idols talk about their daily lives, plans, opinions and behaviour in various real or fictional situations. The aim is to make fans identify with the idols and build idealized images of them. Likewise, these magazines contain extensive coverage of the professional activities of the idols, as well as columns for communication between them and fans through letters. On the covers are always the idols that will release musical productions or participate in a movie or series to premiere that month. The covers allow for the general public's exposure to the idols' images and names because the magazines are typically placed on prominent shelves in Japanese bookstores and convenience stores. On the other hand, the groups on the covers have an average of 2.6 extra pages in their regular section within the magazine, in addition to sometimes appearing in posters attached. Thus, for fans, these magazines are a form of communication with the idols and a collectable item, so they are motivated to buy them monthly.

Diversification and market expansion

The third stage of idol production in Johnny's Jimusho consists of diversifying activities and releasing products to reach new sectors of consumers beyond core fans. These activities focus on acting, hosting radio and television shows, and allowing the idols' particular talents to develop. Although juniors and young idols participate in television shows, movies and stages, once an idol group has established a secure position in the market, its members begin to perform regularly in television, theatre and movies, but they do it in leading roles and the company links their activities to group's products as much as possible. This section relies only on Arashi's case to deconstruct its development and illustrate the process of diversification and expansion that occurred between 2004 and 2010.

As it was previously explained, when the idols make their official debut, they already have experience hosting television programmes because the company promotes these activities through the shows dedicated to juniors. Therefore, the debuted groups usually get regular television and radio shows or become the leading hosts for junior shows. In the case of Arashi, because the Volleyball World Cup and its participation as the promotional personality marked its debut, the group hosted various special shows covering the event. Afterwards, during the first year of its debut, the members were individually assigned as main hosts to weekly radio programmes. They also co-hosted the juniors' weekend afternoon television shows *Gakibara Teigoku 2000!* (TBS) and *USO?! Japan* (TBS), sharing credits with the leader of the juniors at the time – Takizawa Hideaki – and their senior Kokubun Taichi, a member of TOKIO. It was in 2001 when they were assigned their first weekly television show centred on Arashi, *Mayonaka no Arashi* (NTV), which was broadcast past midnight. However, the time slot meant that its audience was limited and composed mainly of fans willing to stay awake or record the show to watch afterwards; this is typical for group-centred shows in their beginnings.

In November 2001, as part of the celebrations for Arashi's second anniversary, Johnny's Jimusho established a recording label – JStorm – to produce all the group's music-related products and even some movies, instead of relying on external producers as they did until then (J Storm Inc n.d.). This was a new strategy that the company proved with Arashi. As a result, in 2002 and 2004, JStorm produced two movies starring the group's five members, with a coming-of-age story centred on friendship and written by another Inohara Yoshihiko, a member of the senior group V6: *PIKANCHI Life Is Hard Dakedo Happy* and *PIKANCHI Life Is Hard Dakara Happy*. Their respective theme songs were sung by Arashi and released as the singles *PIKANCHI* and *PIKANCHI Double*. As can be seen, by this strategy, Johnny's Jimusho created numerous products related to the group, which also increased the visibility of the members.[3]

In 2004, Arashi and the members individually worked to diversify and expand their audience by consolidating each member's personality and the group's symbolism. In spring, Aiba Masaki began co-hosting a weekend family television show, *Tensai! Shimura Dōbutsuen* (NTV).[4] This programme became popular because it focused on presenting the *tarento* interacting with various animals. Aiba went to zoos and animal centres in Japan and other parts of the world to help take care of animals and show the audience more about them. He was regularly shown getting scratched and lightly bitten by lions, tigers, kangaroos and other exotic animals or bathing and caring for abandoned or sick dogs and cats. However, he was always smiling, considerate of animals and people, and willing to follow the experts' instructions. As a result, his personality became widely known as easy-going, humble, funny and sociable. Although he was the only member of Arashi participating in this programme, he constantly talked about the group or shared anecdotes about other members. Moreover, because its primary audience included children and their parents, the recognition for him and Arashi within that market sector grew.

Then, during the summer, the broadcaster NTV selected Arashi to sing the image song – *HERO* – for its coverage of the 2004 Olympic Games. This gave the group a chance to be heard by audiences not regularly exposed to idols' music. Furthermore, the same broadcaster designated it as the leading personality and host of the annual charity programme *24-hour TV*. This is an event of national impact for its focus on strengthening the feeling of community among Japanese people; each year, NTV selects a popular *tarento* to act as an ambassador of the cause and retain the audience's attention during the 24-hour live broadcast during which the organizers receive people's donations (Nippon Television Network Corporation n.d.). Thus, this show is a valuable opportunity for *tarento* to obtain more recognition from the Japanese audience. On this occasion, Arashi performed some songs, the members visited diverse towns in Japan, interacted with locals and spent some time with people with complex illnesses or conditions; at the climax of the broadcasting, they read letters to express how much the rest of the members and Arashi meant to them. Through this participation, the group showed a socially conscious and more mature image to fans, got other audiences to identify the members as idols and began to be known as a group with a special bond, which became one of its most relevant symbolic traits.

In 2005, Arashi continued with its weekday late-night show that had evolved from *Mayonaka no Arashi* to *D no Arashi* (NTV). Nevertheless, in spring, the group got a regular family-oriented variety show, *Mago mago Arashi* (Fuji

TV), broadcast on Saturdays at 1.00 pm. In this, the members visited regular families to spend a day with them, taking the role of grandchildren to older couples or childminders and cooks to couples with children that needed help; some other segments showed them taking Mandarin lessons, visiting castles in Japan and even cleaning them. The programme ran for two and a half years and had 125 episodes. This show allowed Arashi to be known by children and adults not regularly interested in idols. It also reinforced the group's social appeal by presenting the members caring for regular people when performing daily routines with their host families, from helping older people with their businesses or accompanying them in their hobbies to changing the diapers of children.

Continuing with their diversification, in 2006, Sakurai Sho – the only member with a bachelor's degree[5] – became a regular anchor in a weekday night news programme, *News Zero* (NTV). This achievement allowed him to break the stereotype of an idol entirely, present himself to mature social sectors and get this audience to know about Arashi because he and his co-hosts regularly commented about the group's activities as part of the cultural section of the news. Also, Sakurai opened a niche for younger Johnny's idols who followed his example of going to university and, eventually, were recruited for various news shows. On the other hand, in 2008, Ohno Satoshi, who continuously shared that his hobbies were drawing and sculpting, opened an exhibition in Tokyo, *Freestyle*, gaining recognition from other artists and media.

Another important activity of debuted idols to reach broader audiences is acting. As seen in Table 5, from before their debut to 2010, the overall participation of Arashi's members as main actors showed more than a threefold increase in annual averages, while secondary roles significantly reduced. Most of the plays, series and films in which the group's members participated were not produced by Johnny's Jimusho, which implies the diversity of genres and, consequently, of target audiences. Likewise, the participation of actors and actresses unrelated to the company can potentially attract audiences unfamiliar with Johnny's idols. In the case of stage plays, these are typically limited to Tokyo and Osaka venues, but television and film productions have a national reach; in some cases, they may even get to worldwide audiences, although they are not the target. These last types of productions also boost the actor's recognition as a member of an idol group and promote its products through music singles that are used as theme, opening or ending songs. In the case of Arashi, 76 per cent of the singles released from 1999 to 2010 were related to series or movies in which at least one of the members was the leading actor.

All this involves the idols and the groups exposing themselves to new audiences. Similarly, the constant participation of the members in different types of productions, the success of these and the recognition received from different media for their performances create expectations towards their subsequent works. This is evident in the case of Arashi and shows its evolution from a regular Johnny's idol unit to a national idol group, which will be discussed in the next chapter.

For example, between October and December 2005, Matsumoto Jun had one of the leading roles in the romantic youth television series *Hana yori dango* (TBS), which obtained an average rating of 19.80 and received various popularity awards. In her study about Japanese television, Lukács (2010: 214) identified that, during the second half of the 1990s, a rating of 15 and above was a hit and above 20 points represented a mega-hit. However, during the 2000s, market fragmentation increased, and the average ratings progressively declined. Therefore, this series was a mega-hit that the producers exploited for

Table 5 Arashi's acting activities until 2010.

Category	1995–1999 (pre-debut)		2000–2010	
	In the period	**Annual average**	**In the period**	**Annual average**
Plays with a member as the leading actor	2	0.5	15	1.5
Plays with a member as a secondary actor	1	0.3	1	0.1
TV series with a member as the leading actor	6	1.5	59	5.9
TV series with a member as a secondary actor	8	2	13	1.3
Movies with a member as the leading actor	1	0.3	14	1.4
Movies with a member as a secondary actor	0	0	1	0.1

Source: Elaborated by the author.

a second season broadcast between January and March 2007. This surpassed the first season, obtaining an average rating of 21.70 that prompted the production of a movie released in June 2008, becoming one of the top ten highest-grossing movies at the box office that year (Box Office Mojo 2009).[6] The franchise of *Hana yori dango* meant a considerable expansion in the popularity of Matsumoto and Arashi among Japanese and Asian audiences, which were familiar with the story from its original manga version and a Taiwanese live-action series. In 2007, Matsumoto also starred in a series about Italian cooking, *Bambino!* (NTV), which got an average rating of 14.2 and received an award for his performance. Arashi was the interpreter of the main theme songs used in the four productions, which were sold as singles. The relevance of all the strategies translates into the performance of these in the music market. *Wish* – the theme song of *Hana yori dango* got first place in sales during the week of release; *Love so sweet* and *One love* – the theme songs for the second season and movie – got into the top five best-selling singles of 2007 and 2008, respectively (Recording Industry Association of Japan 2006, 2008, 2009).

Ninomiya Kazunari was another member consolidating his acting career and supporting Arashi's recognition and broadening of audiences. In early 2006, he starred in a television drama, *Sukoshi wa ongaeshi ga dekinakata* (TBS), playing a young man with cancer. The drama scored a rating of 14.60, and his performance earned him a national award and the audience's praise. That year, he also got one of the leading roles in *Letters from Iwo Jima*, a film directed by Clint Eastwood about the Second World War. These two roles consolidated Ninomiya as an actor and got him recognition for the challenging roles and his disposition to sacrifice his idol image. In 2007, he starred in a family series, *Haikei Chichiuesama* (Fuji TV), which averaged a 13.20 rating; in another drama in which he played a young man with health problems, *Marathon* (TBS), that scored a 15.20 rating; and, along with Sakurai, a teenage romantic series, *Yamada Taro Monogatari* (TBS), which averaged a rating of 15.20. Again, he received awards for his performances, which facilitated that more mature audiences and teenagers – who were the primary audience of those stories – knew about Arashi.

In 2007, Arashi's special group activities continued parallel to those of the members. First, the group participated in another movie produced by JStorm,

Kiiroi namida; similar to the *Pikanchi* stories, it focused on friendship and the pursuit of dreams but as young adults in the 1960s. In 2008, the group was selected for a second time as the leading host and personality for the *24-hour TV* (NTV) charity event. At the end of the year, Arashi's three singles reached the annual top ten, including first place (Recording Industry Association of Japan 2009).

Finally, despite diversifying activities and market segments, Johnny's Jimusho ensures the groups' core performances as idols: concerts. Arashi held an annual tour from 2002 onwards, visiting some of the main cities of Japan. However, it wasn't until 2006 that the group made its first visit to other countries through the *Jet Storm* campaign, holding press conferences in Taiwan, Thailand and South Korea in one day. Then, in September, the group held its tour *ARASHI AROUND ASIA* with concerts in Taipei, Bangkok and Seoul. Interestingly, contrary to the strategies of Korean artists who were entering the Japanese market performing entirely in the Japanese language, the members of Arashi only learned to introduce themselves in the local languages and sang a couple of representative songs of the group in Korean, Chinese and Thai, but their interaction with fans and the rest of the performances were in Japanese. In 2007, Arashi held its first concert at the Tokyo Dome. Then, in 2008, the group held a national dome tour and a second Asian tour that opened with a concert at the largest venue in Japan – the Kasumigaoka National Stadium[7] – that continued with concerts in Taipei, Seoul and Shanghai. The media in Japan covered the Asian tour enthusiastically, stressing Arashi's popularity in the region and the impact the group had in motivating Asian fans to learn Japanese. For the next three years, for the tenth anniversary tour *5 × 10* and the tour *Scene*, Arashi had shows at the Kasumigaoka Stadium.

The concerts are essential for diversifying and consolidating markets for various reasons. First, they represent the most direct contact of the groups with fans, which is a relationship that idols must nurture continuously. Second, in financial terms, the tours mean direct revenue for the tickets sold and indirect revenues because they are one of the main motivations for fans to pay their annual membership to the fan club, as explained before. Third, the company further profits from the concerts by releasing them on DVD and Blu-Ray in various versions, as done with the singles and albums, motivating the fans to acquire them regardless of whether they have assisted or not. In Arashi's case, the tours' videos released since 2007, when the group consolidated and rapidly expanded its market, were the top-selling videos annually (Recording Industry Association of Japan 2008, 2009, 2010, 2011).

The success of these strategies in expanding the consumer base for an idol group is evident in the surveys that the annual music show *Best Artist* (NTV) used to present before the artists' performances, revealing the sex and age range of the audience who had voted for each one. In 2003, before Arashi began an accelerated diversification of activities, the voters were primarily women between seven and forty-nine years old and teenage boys; however, in 2011 – the last year that the show presented those graphs – more than a quarter of voters were male of various ages.

Symbolism and upgraded strategies

The intensive and extensive exposure of Johnny's idols in Japanese media promotes in the audience a sense of familiarity and intimacy with them because their narratives are presented as if their private and public personas concur. Of course, this does not mean that they do not present divergences in their personality, but those are elements considered part of the *omote/ura* and *honne/tatemae* naturalized as part of the Japanese people's ethos. For example, the idols typically deny any romantic relationship – so they do not offend the fans' sensibilities – but when they marry or have a child, they summon press conferences or release written statements. In these cases, the audience and media do not accuse the idols of having lied before for not admitting they had a partner because it is understood that it was part of their *ura*.

This does not mean that tabloids, mainly those not related to mainstream media corporations, continuously expose allegedly secret information, but there is a close collaboration between the major media corporations and Johnny's Jimusho to keep under control the gossip that is presented on television; this allows the idols to remain relatively protected from scandals that could ruin their symbolic value and careers (West 2006). This is the case because their socially proper image is essential to maintaining a successful Japanese entertainment career. Johnny's idols can have relatively rebellious images regarding fashion or tastes but not behaviours that are the basis of

Japanese social harmony. If they misbehave, they must apologize to the audiences, the media and the corporations they represent for offending them and remain outside the public eye for some time as a punishment (Marx 2012; West 2006).

The symbolic production of the idols as image commodities to feed the imagination of the audience is encouraged by the media narrative of *honne-ni-semaru* (addressing the honest opinions) during interviews, in which the topics they talk about are primarily *urabanashi* (inside stories) or their opinions on everyday issues and their personal lives, like family, friends, work struggles, love ideals. Evidently, this information may appear irrelevant to the casual observer; however, for the regular audience, particularly fans, those details are high-value information to feed their fantasies and put together the pieces to complete the whole picture of the idols' lives and personalities. In terms of symbolic construction, this *honne*-giving narrative allows them to be perceived as an ordinary person with the same struggles, dreams and values as any other Japanese. At the same time, it builds a *sugao/sunao* (honest) aura that is particularly valued by the audience.

Therefore, Johnny's Jimusho carefully chooses the type of productions for its idols, controls the information published about them, and monitors the activities and people they relate with in their private lives to guarantee the congruence of their images and narratives and keep the affective bond with the audience, which enables the acceptance of the discourses they represent. This also satisfies most fans, so they respect the idols' private life. For example, Johnny's fans consider that waiting outside locations or studios is acceptable because it is part of the idols' public activities and gives fans a chance to show their support and commitment; however, they do not venture to follow them to their houses because that is a break of the fan code, and the fan community protects the idols from *okakke* fans (stalkers).

In the 2000s, Johnny's Jimusho applied aggressive strategies to diversify the activities of its idols and promote them in Japanese society beyond teenagers, who were the typical consumers of idols in previous decades. Instead of relying only on musical productions, series and movies targeted at young audiences, the company promoted for its idols to polish their talents and social abilities to display them in a variety of content aimed at broader audiences. Then, these would support and grow the regular consumer base – fans – and reflect on the success of their musical productions. In this way, Johnny's idols have dominated the Japanese music industry since the end of the decade. The relevance that the company's idols have acquired is perceived in the seasonal specials of the music shows across broadcasters, like *Premium Music* (NTV), *The Music Day* (NTV), *Best Artist* (NTV), *FNS Kayōsai* (Fuji TV) and *Music Station* (Asahi TV). In these, Johnny's groups dominate the time onscreen by having regular performances and collaborations among them, which are highly celebrated by the audience.

Furthermore, by diversifying their activities, Johnny's idols have matured in the entertainment industry and become respected actors and hosts, allowing them to prolong their careers well into their forties. Thus, their significance has crossed the music realm; they have become part of the Japanese society landscape and are recognized as such by mainstream media, which benefit from having them in their productions. Relevant examples of this integration of Johnny's Jimusho with mainstream media corporations are the cases of the annual Johnny's Countdown and the shows at the public broadcaster NHK. Since 1998, Johnny's Jimusho has produced a collective concert to receive the new year – called *Johnny's Countdown* – at the Tokyo Dome during the last hour of December and the first of January. Tickets for this concert can be acquired only by members of the official fan clubs and are highly pursued by fans because this is one of the few opportunities to see all the idols of the company in one place and receive the year with them. The demand from fans nationwide to have access to this concert made it easy for the company to sell the rights to Fuji TV for live broadcasting. Every year, fifteen minutes before midnight, the concert broadcast begins, and fans can follow the show and the countdown for the new year with their favourite idols (Fuji TV n.d.). On the other hand, besides *The Shonen Club* focused on Johnny's juniors, NHK began producing *The Shonen Club Premium* in 2006. This is a monthly 1-hour show in which debuted idols are the host; it is focused on the latest productions, musical numbers and interviews with the debuted idols (NHK n.d.b).

By the end of the 2010s, with the changing trends of media consumption in Japan, the promotional strategies for Johnny's idols have adapted. Since the mid-2010s, there has been a rapid migration of young adults and teenagers from television to streaming services in Japan, which reached people in their thirties and forties during the pandemic; YouTube became the most popular social media platform in Japan, followed by LINE, Twitter, Instagram, Facebook and TikTok (Digital Business Lab 2022; Hotaka and Asoda 2021; Saito 2020). Therefore, it is no surprise that, since 2019, beginning with Arashi, the idols have opened their official YouTube and other social media accounts, releasing special versions of music videos and interacting with fans through live appearances on those platforms. This move has not affected the selling numbers of physical CDs, DVDs and Blu-rays; on the contrary, Johnny's groups have kept the top places on the selling lists in all domestic categories (Recording Industry Association of Japan 2020, 2021, 2022, 2023a). This is because the free official material on the internet has not replaced the traditional strategies of releasing unique material and special versions only available in the physical products, which are extremely valuable for fans, particularly when those are known to become scarce, like when a group announces its retirement or when the fans are trying to show their support to a group by helping them break records, which will be analysed in the following chapters.

The national idols and their role to strengthen social ties in Japan

More than a century ago, Durkheim (2012) recognized that modern societies could establish themselves as sacred through the sentiment of patriotism and the rituals of nationalism, which transformed the homeland into the entity that moved the masses into common aims guided by states, replacing the symbolic power of a god. In the new millennium, globalization, the growing power of multinational capitals and the impact of culturally diverse waves of immigrants have weakened states' ability to direct societies to common goals (Smith 2007: 27). Nowadays, nationalism appeals more to identity than political ideology, and national identities are deeply embodied in contemporary societies as a dominant criterion of identification, giving people emotional attachments, values and beliefs to get through life (Delanty 1999; Kelman 2011). These are transmitted formally through educational systems to the members of the nation but also by processes of cultural and banal nationalism that focus on the reproduction of patriotic sentiments and consciousness through culture; also, these movements do not seek political actions *per se* but aim to instil a nationalist ideology for the support of the state (Kelman 2011).

Cultural nationalism movements are expected when the national identity is perceived as weak or threatened. They are usually led by the intelligentsia, relying on an upgraded set of ideas and principles about the nation's uniqueness that aims to strengthen the people's attachment towards the nation-state (Yoshino 2005). On the other hand, banal nationalism is a process of constant, unmindful and casual *flagging* or display of symbols and narratives that condense nationhood as a continuous reminder of their belonging to one nation; it simultaneously stimulates memory and forgetting to naturalize habits and beliefs in people's minds (Billig 1995). Just as physical flags, the symbols and narratives of nationhood are waved seeking a conscious response from people, like a respectful salute or deep emotions; or, they can appear unwaved, as part of everyday life, but because of their pervasiveness and ability to interpellate people, they reinforce the existence of the nation 'mindlessly, rather than mindfully' (Billig 1995: 38). In contemporary nation-states, the media is the most powerful tool to achieve this. Nevertheless, no content can attain something by simply presenting a message; for it to be effective, people must be interpellated (Barthes 1977). In this sense, celebrities – which are pervasive in contemporary societies – have become relevant instruments to propagate national ideologies.

In the case of Japanese society and its national identity, the twentieth century was challenging. It began under the *fukoku kyōhei* policy (rich country, strong army), which made it a national goal to work diligently to turn Japan into the leader of Asia. On this aim, the state heavily promoted the development of a strong national identity through the educational system and the army; it was centred on symbols such as the Imperial and Shinto institutions, the anthem and the flag and the national pride (Gordon 2003; Iida 2002). As history shows, this took a turn for the worst, inspiring the ultra-nationalist militarism that concluded with the defeat of Japan in the Pacific War. The Japanese people and their leaders had to deal with rebuilding their country under the guidance of their previous enemies. At the same time, their national symbols were stigmatized, and they had to deny all virtue to their traditional values.

In the 1960s, Japan was enjoying economic growth, but the national identity lingered in uncertainty with no concrete symbols to be attached to, and civil movements and some radical demonstrations threatened the social stability (Kurokawa 2010; Morris-Suzuki 2006; Toriyama and Buist 2003; Upham 1993). Intellectual elites' answer to restoring a robust national identity that was not related to militarism was to promote a cultural nationalist movement focused on repeating to the Japanese people – and the rest of the world – the supposedly unique characteristics they had and claiming that these were the reason of their economic success. This movement and discourse was popularly identified as *Nihonjinron*, and was supported by the government, turning it into a hegemonic ideology that was highly instructive on the behaviour and attitudes expected from the Japanese people; the success of implanting this ideology in the Japanese people's minds has made some analysts consider it a civil religion (Befu 2001; Iida 2002; Yoshino 2005). According to a quinquennial survey to measure value orientations among Japanese people aged sixteen and over, in 1973, 60 per cent of people considered that their national qualities were superior to those of other nationalities; however, in 1983, after a decade of strong *Nihonjinon* discourses in media, 70 per cent of respondents agreed on that sentence (Kei, Koichi and Miwako 2010).

Nevertheless, the economic downturns of the 1990s and 2000s once again weakened Japanese society's cohesion; young people were blamed for not sacrificing enough for the collective, and women for not wanting to get married and have children (Uno 1993; Yamada 1999). This is reflected in the sentiments of young people. For example, in the survey of 1998, the respondents between sixteen and twenty-nine years old were the ones with the lowest confidence in the Japanese intrinsical qualities as being superior, with only 25 per cent agreeing with that sentence (Kei, Koichi and Miwako 2010: 44). Thus, the Japanese society seemed to have lost something to be proud of while watching its Asian neighbours grow stronger. Still, in the 2000s, the popularity of Japanese media products – anime, manga and video games – around the world inspired the government to move the national identity discourse to cultural products. After the Great Eastern Japan Earthquake of 2011, the government and industry leaders began a highly ideological campaign following the premises of the *Nihonjinron* to strengthen social ties (*kizuna*), which became a form of banal nationalism supported by some idols from Johnny's Jimusho that represent traditional values and interpellate Japanese audiences (Mandujano 2014a; Mandujano-Salazar 2018a).

As sociologist Alexander (2010) says, some celebrities achieve the status of icons in contemporary societies, mediating between an aesthetic structure that induces audiences' attachment and their most profound emotional needs and moral ideals. Thus, this chapter analyses the role of three idol groups in this process, focusing on the label of *kokuminteki aidoru* or national idols that media used to refer to them, and stressing their discursive and representational characteristics and how these can be related to national identity ideology in moments of crises or distress.

SMAP, the national star

SMAP – short for Spots Music Assemble People – debuted in 1991 and was formed by six adolescents who had been back dancers for the older Johnny's groups, like Hikaru GENJI: Nakai Masahiro, Kimura Takuya, Inagaki Goro, Kusanagi Tsuyoshi, Katori Shingo and Mori Katsuyuki. Although the first years were not particularly positive regarding the selling numbers of the group's singles and albums, SMAP would mark a turning point for Johnny's Jimusho and the social relevance of its idols in Japan. To promote the group beyond the musical shows that also included those more famous artists, the company applied the strategies seen in the previous chapter and arranged the inclusion of SMAP in variety shows. The first variety of the group was *Ai rabu SMAP*[1] (TV Tokyo). It was a teenager-oriented show aimed primarily at female fans; it allowed each member's personality to show and supported the recognition of some of Johnny's juniors. In 1992, the group also became part of the regular *tarento* appearing in a late-night variety show called *Yume ga MORI MORI* (Fuji TV), in which the members performed sketches, sometimes putting themselves in comical situations not usual for idols at the time, gaining them some recognition among other audiences.

Then, on 17 January 1995, Japan suffered one of the deadliest natural disasters of that century in the form of the Great Hanshin Earthquake that left thousands of people homeless and buildings damaged in the area of Kobe and Awaji Island (Fukushima 1995). That year, SMAP was chosen as the leading personality for the *24-hour TV* (NTV) charity show, resulting in the first time that one of Johnny's groups led a national interest event. The members were shown in the disaster region, talking and caring for victims; they presented not as unreachable stars but as relatable young Japanese men that used their popularity and vigour to help strengthen their community's unity, or *kizuna*. The collaboration of the company and the charity show was so successful for both parties that, from then on, every year – except in 1996 and 1999 – some group or individual idol from Johnny's has acted as the main personality to attract audiences (Nippon Television Network Corporation n.d.).[2]

In 1996, SMAP got to host its own variety show aimed at general adult audiences during the prime-time slot on Mondays from 10.00 pm to 10.54 pm: *SMAPxSMAP* (Fuji TV). This show rapidly became a national-level hit that broadcast until the group's disbandment. It relied on SMAP's high-quality parodies and the members cooking gourmet and international recipes, performing their singles, and interviewing and performing in collaboration with national and international stars. Mori retired from the group that year, and SMAP became a quintet.

In the following years, the participation of the five members in numerous films and television series gained the group more recognition. In particular, Kimura Takuya starred in numerous highly popular romantic series, like *Long Vacation* (Fuji TV) and *Love Generation* (Fuji TV), which got average ratings of over 26 per cent and gave him the status of *the* Japanese heartthrob of the time. On the other hand, Nakai was recognized for his abilities as a host; in 1997, he was chosen as one for the *Kōhaku Uta Gassen* (NHK), which was another first for Johnny's Jimusho and its involvement in national events. SMAP's popularity increased beyond usual teenage fans; in 1998, its single *Yozora no Mukō* sold more than a million copies and, in 2000, *Lion Heart* became a 2-million hit (Recording Industry Association of Japan 2001).

For best and for worst, SMAP and its members became recognizable stars. Consequently, when some personal issues became public, they turned into the gossip of the moment. At the end of 2000, Kimura announced that he was marrying the idol Kudo Shizuka and they would become parents. A married idol was not something expected at the time, so the first reaction of the media and fans was a worry that he would soon retire. However, after the official press release, Kimura and the company were careful to keep any other information and image of him as a husband or father away from the mainstream media and official content related to him. Minor gossip media released, from time to time, articles and photographs of Kimura and Kudo, but they were not covered on television, so they did not have a significant impact on the image of Kimura or SMAP, allowing him to keep his role as a sex symbol and SMAP's popularity.

Nonetheless, in 2001, Inagaki was arrested for trying to flee in his car from a police officer and, in the attempt, causing her a minor injury. Because this was an offence against the law, all media covered the issue, and Inagaki, through Johnny's Jimusho, had to release a statement to apologize and explain the incident; he received a punishment of five months in house arrest; during this time, his image was retired from all media, including publicity campings he endorsed. The other four members had to finish a national tour without him, and they decided to withdraw from that year's *Kōhaku Uta Gassen* (NHK). Even so, SMAP appealed to the fans' support, promising them to become a better group. Inagaki rejoined the group in January 2002 at the *SMAPxSMAP* episode with the highest rating in its history – 34.2 – and sang meaningful songs about friendship and the importance of strengthening ties (*kizuna*) among people (Forbridge 2016). This way, Johnny's Jimusho and SMAP used the incident to reinforce a narrative of the importance of collectiveness and social support against adversity that resonated with traditional discourses of *Nihonjinron*; Ingaki obtained the social pardon and recovered his popularity.

In 2002, almost as an affirmation of such pardon, SMAP's single *Yozora no Mukō* was chosen to be included in the middle-school music textbooks, giving the group more national recognition. The following year, the group's single *Sekai ni hitotsu dake no hana,* which was an anthem to self-forgiveness and the value of every human being's uniqueness, became a 3-million hit and one the best-selling singles of all time in Japan (Recording Industry Association of Japan 2004); this gained the group the honour to be the closing act at that year's *Kōhaku Uta Gassen* (NHK). Then, in 2005, SMAP performed at the National Olympic Stadium in Tokyo, becoming the first artist ever to hold a concert there (The Huffington Post 2014). Then, in 2008, two other songs of the group were added to high-school textbooks.

Therefore, despite their new albums and singles not selling anything close to the million mark, the five members, already in their thirties, had the status of national-level stars. However, in 2009, Kusanagi was arrested for being caught drunk and naked at a public park. As expected in a situation that was a criminal offence, it immediately became national breaking news. He had to send a public apology, show remorse and disappear from the media for some time (J-Cast News 2009; Senju 2017; Sugiyama 2020). The opportunity for SMAP to repay the public debt came in 2011, when, along with other Johnny's groups, the members were deeply involved in charity activities to support the Great Eastern Japan Earthquake victims. When Johnny's Jimusho launched the *Marching J* project, SMAP joined the rest of the company's younger idols and met fans to encourage people to donate (Oricon News 2011a).

In August 2011, SMAP held its first concert overseas, performing in Beijing for 70,000 fans under the theme: 'Do your best, Japan. Thank you, China. Asia is one.' This was a gratitude expression from Japan to China for its support after the earthquake (CNTV 2011). Such cultural exchange was reported as a soft-power action from Japan and China to relieve the political tensions that had been intensifying between both countries (BBC News 2011). Also, the idea of Asia as one implied the notion of *kizuna* among the Asian community.

On 14 August 2016, after twenty-five years as a debuted group, SMAP announced its disbandment by the end of the year. This was the major national news for almost a week; hard-news programmes and morning shows analysed the repercussions that this would mean for Japanese media. Regardless of the minor offences over the years, in the numerous recounts of the history of the group, the media call it *kokuminteki star* (national star) and *kokuminteki aidoru* (national idol) while stressing how SMAP had marked an era in Japanese entertainment; it was also highlighted the fact that the members had surpassed the typical idol roles, maturing in front of the audience and lifting the national spirit in moments of crises (Kikuchi 2016; Kurihara 2016). Interestingly, the title of a national idol was first used, in the case of Johnny's Jimusho, with Arashi, but it was SMAP's trajectory the one that opened the path for this and the rest of the company's groups to achieve national-level relevance.

Arashi, the ambassador of Japaneseness

In 2008, as seen in the previous chapter, Arashi – with the five members in their twenties – was beginning to dominate the Japanese music scene and have a presence in all media and a variety of content, appealing to younger and older people. That year, the group was embarking on its second Asian tour with concerts in Taipei, Seoul and Shanghai (Johnny & Associates 2023a), while SMAP was having image troubles and not selling as well as in previous years. More importantly, amid the Korean Wave, a very young Korean idol quintet – TVXQ, which debuted in Japan in 2005 with the name Tohoshinki – was gaining recognition and representing a threat to the dominance of Johnny's Jimusho in the male-idol market. Avex domestically produced Tohoshinki, and the members sang and interacted in Japanese. By 2008, its growing success gained the group an invitation to participate in the *Kōhaku Uta Gassen* (NHK), which Arashi would achieve until the following year. In 2009, Tohoshinki's popularity continued growing along with the selling numbers of its singles, albums and videos listed as domestic productions and competing directly with Arashi and other Johnny's idols (Recording Industry Association of Japan 2009, 2010). At this time, the Japanese media began to apply the *kokuminteki aidoru* (national idol) label to Arashi and its members. This circumstance can be interpreted as a strategy from Johnny's Jimusho and the Japanese media corporations that depended on Johnny's idols to deal with and differentiate from the foreign competition. Nonetheless, this tactic soon became more ideological in the context of cultural promotion policies from the Japanese government.

In 2009, the media began to use recurrent narratives and representations of the five members of Arashi that stressed their qualities as idols and national ambassadors of specific values and masculinity. In their typical work – variety and music shows, idol magazine interviews, series and movies – the media emphasized idol symbolism, like their approachability, friendship among the members, physical attractiveness and masculinity, implicitly suggesting that such features were national ideals. Furthermore, in the content related to issues of an evident social impact, like charity and tourism campaigns, their qualities as Japanese ambassadors were highlighted but supported by Arashi's attractiveness and ability to get broad attention from inside and outside Japan. For instance, in June 2010's issue of the men's magazine *GQ Japan*, the cover story presented the group posing in white and grey suits with a heading proclaiming: 'The day the national idols become the genuine good men' (Tatsuta 2010). This magazine also awarded three of the five members the title of *GQ Men of the Year* between 2008 and 2011 and featured all of them in different numbers.[3] As a result of getting incessantly attached to their names and images and the label of national idols, Arashi achieved more respect and recognition among the entire society; their media activities attracted attention, and people seemed to relate quality to everything they endorsed.

In 2010, the METI established the Cool Japan Office to be in charge of the planning and applying of policies to promote creative industries – media products and contents, architecture, antiques, crafts, publishing, computer software and services, furniture, jewellery, food and tourism – facilitating its expansion inside and outside Japan (Creative Industries Division Ministry of Economy Trade and Industry 2012; Keisai Sangyōshō 2021). The logic behind these policies also included a strategy for cultural promotion. The economic, governmental and industrial elites relied on the Japanese cultural appeal to attract international consumers and increase the value of the country's brand (Valaskivi 2013). At the same time, the Ministry of Land Infrastructure Transport and Tourism (MLIT) was also launching a cultural promotion campaign that counted on the close cooperation with cultural producers and media corporations, in which Arashi had a central role. That spring, the Japan Tourism Agency (JTA), part of the MLIT, designated Arashi as *Kankō Rikkoku Navigator* (Navigator for National Tourism) to act as an ambassador for the campaign *Japan. Endless Discovery.* The official announcement and media reports stressed that Arashi and Johnny's Jimusho were contributing to the whole campaign without any remuneration and stated the expectation that Arashi, in the role of *Nippon no kao* (face of Japan), helped to increase tourism (Kanko Keizai Shinbun 2010; Kankōchō 2010a). Promotional spots began broadcasting in diverse countries of East Asia and the United States, showing Arashi members speaking in Chinese, Korean and English to invite people to visit Japan and enjoy tourism spots and high-quality food and products.

In the following months, the Japanese government, media and Johnny's Jimusho implemented a series of strategies centred on Arashi that constantly flagged national identity elements so that media producers and sponsors could capitalize on the group's status as *national* idols. As an example of this collaboration take the following. In April, the JTA announced that it would join forces with the Tokyo International Airport – commonly known as Haneda – to promote domestic tourism (Kankōchō 2010b). Then, in September, Japan Airlines (JAL), the country's flag airline and one of the primary providers of domestic flights, signed Arashi for its national campaign. As part of this, the members' faces were printed on some of the planes that served three important domestic destinations – Sapporo, Fukuoka and Osaka. The press release by JAL stated that Arashi was chosen for its vast popularity and role as the face of tourism, as well as due to the group and Johnny's Jimusho's intention of spreading joy from Japan to everyone, an aim that the airline said to share (Japan Airlines 2010). The same month, the JTA published a book called *Nippon no Arashi* (*The Arashi of Japan* or, translated literally, *The Storm of Japan*) and distributed it to elementary, middle and high schools in Japan with the explicit objective of promoting among young generations the love for their country and the motivation to work for its improvement (Kankōchō 2010c).

The book followed the style and narrative of typical idol photobooks, heavily relying on candid-looking photographs of Arashi. However, instead of being in studio locations, they were in real locations around the country and, in some pictures, they were interacting with ordinary Japanese people or crafters. The narrative focused on rediscovering Japan. The book included essays – purportedly – written by the members and their conversations with the people in the photographs; in these, they expressed their admiration for Japanese people and stressed the value of Japan's nature, traditions and culture. These sentiments appeared eloquently in paragraphs like the following:

> Right now, we must be truly proud of ourselves as Japanese people. In Japan, where we live, there are many kind and sincere people. It has become difficult to see that in urban daily life. This is why we took a trip to reencounter those people [...] We believe we can produce a storm of kindness in Japan.[4]
>
> (Arashi 2011: 9)

Hence, the domestic tourism campaign relied on the collaboration of the government, media, industry producers and Johnny's Jimusho with Arashi as the focus, accompanied by a soft patriotic narrative. Nevertheless, the Great Eastern Japan Earthquake of 2011 encouraged this campaign and Arashi's ideological role to be significantly reinforced. Promptly after the disaster, the government formed a Cool Japan Advisory Council (CJAC) with representatives of the ministries, industry, media and scholars; they released a document with the meaningful title *Creating a New Japan Tying together 'Culture and Industry' and 'Japan and the world'* (Cool Japan Advisory Council 2011).[5] The proposed plan was precise in its aim to reinforce the Japanese identity in a context of recovery and overcoming of challenges:

> Japan must work quickly to dispel any short-term negative impact to its image by supplying information accurately and immediately. It must then continuously tell the world of the unshakably strong qualities of Japan and comprehensively engage in proactive public relations that highlight Japan's recovery. Moreover, as the world's concern focuses on Japan, it must also send out messages that utilize the power of sympathy and feelings of gratitude.
>
> (Cool Japan Advisory Council 2011: 7)

Promptly, the national media and corporations started numerous projects supported by a patriotic discourse that stressed Japanese people's solidarity, sacrifice, resilience and strength, and the importance of their love for their nation to be translated into actions aimed at common interests. One of the strategies to support this discourse, the value of Japan's brand and the tourism campaign was the postulation of Tokyo as a candidate to host the 2020 Olympics. The bidding campaign that invaded Japanese media and landscape from late 2011 until late 2013, when Tokyo won, was built around communicating Japan's strength to the world (Tokyo 2020 Candidate City 2011). Nye (2011), the theorist behind the concept of soft power, visited Japan after the earthquake and wrote that the disaster resulted in a stimulus for Japan's soft power. Indeed, this was the goal of the Japanese elites. On 19 June 2013, the Diet promulgated an act to establish the Japan Brand Fund to advance the development of Japan's attractiveness and the 'unique' characteristics of Japanese culture into new businesses (Ministry of Economy Trade and Industry 2013).

In this context, the members of Arashi, in their roles as national idols and ambassadors of Japanese tourism, swiftly took a leading part in the domestic ideological campaign and media efforts to lessen the survivors' tragedies and focus the society on keeping optimism and working through the strengthening of the country. Arashi was part of the project *Marching J* with other Johnny's Jimusho idols, but the members also helped to clean the disaster area and talked to victims through diverse individual and group projects. In addition, they cheered the Japanese people in general by giving free concerts in the affected areas and performing in other parts of the country at fundraisers to make people aware of the victims' needs. One of these events, *Waku waku gakkō*, was not a concert but a gathering with fans in which the idols performed as school teachers, educating the audience about diverse topics (Nikkan Sports 2011). This event was very successful and well-received by the fans, so it became part of Arashi's yearly events until 2019. Each year, the main topic differed and had an ideological aim: the importance of taking care of the environment, the Japanese traditions, the four seasons of Japan, friendship, etcetera.

Several of the advertising campaigns Arashi or the members endorsed were also filled with messages related to the national purpose of community and rebuilding and the *kizuna* – bonds, ties or connections – among Japanese people. It was as if companies turned to Arashi to promote their products and services to be able to use that narrative. Therefore, commercial advertising and ideological promotion were intertwined. For instance, one of the first special events that Arashi held after the earthquake was a performance collaborating with Disney characters during the group's weekly show *Himitsu no Arashi-chan* (TBS), broadcast on 31 March 2011. Arashi had endorsed the theme park Tokyo Disney Sea since 2009, but on this occasion, the performance explicitly aimed at cheering up Japanese families – while implicitly promoting the theme park. In a very festive musical piece, the group and the Disney characters sang and danced together Disney – not Arashi – songs in front of the studio audience. At the end of the performance, Matsumoto expressed gratitude to the Disney characters, saying that such collaboration had lifted his spirit and hoped it had the same effect on the audience.

Then, in April, the group performed in a special concert produced by the NHK called *Uta de tsunagō* (*Let us connect through songs*); the members' reiterative message throughout their performance was that they believed in the strength of Japan. The same month, AU KDDI – a company of mobile phones endorsed by Arashi – released a television spot in which the idols praised the Japanese people for being 'gentle, hardworking and a bit shy'. Then, on June 30, *The Arashi of Japan,* previously distributed by the JTA to schools, was published to be sold and raise funds for the earthquake victims (Oricon News 2011b). Then, in July, the JTA produced and broadcast the video *Message from Japan* on the Japan National Tourism Organization Website and big screens in 133 countries.[6] This video presented the five members of Arashi expressing their gratitude for the support their country was receiving from around the world; it also emphasized that Japanese people were eager to show their traditions and spirit to the world.

Moreover, Arashi's unreleased song *furusato* (hometown), which the group introduced as part of its participation as Master of Ceremony of 2010's *Kōhaku Uta Gassen* (NHK), was promoted by the public broadcaster as an anthem for national bonding and pride. The lyrics of the song flag the Japanese people's alleged personality qualities and aesthetic sense, as well as the national imagery, as demonstrated by this translated extract:

Because there are rainy days, a rainbow appears; because we face hardships, we become stronger. We have the path we have walked and the map of our dreams in our hearts. [...] That is our hometown.

The people we want to meet are there spreading their kindness and waiting for us. The mountains, the wind and the colour of the sea; this is the place where we can be ourselves. [...] This is my hometown; this is our hometown.[7]

In 2012, the magazine *Nikkei Entertainment* published an article about the impact of Arashi's transformation from a national idol into a Japanese ambassador, stressing the group's strategy of becoming global by staying in Japan (Kimura 2012). In the interview, the members expressed that they considered it more valuable in the current context to get to know more about their own country and contribute to its improvement than aiming to conquer foreign markets.

In 2013, Arashi was once again selected as the leading personality and host of the *24-hour TV* (NTV). The event's theme was boldly expressed on this occasion: 'Japan ... ? The shape of this country.' During the broadcast in which Arashi was designated, the members explained their intention to use the opportunity of the event to reflect along with the audience on their nation and themselves as Japanese. Additionally, the promotional spot showed the idols in different situations depicting purported typical Japanese behaviour. The acting was accompanied by a narrator describing the behaviour and reinforcing the national spirit with the words: 'Japanese people, give your best. For the sake of Japanese people.'

The peak of the explicit national narrative around Arashi was in 2015. This year's event *Waku Waku Gakkō* had as the main topic the Japanese culture expressed during the four seasons. The members taught fans about traditions such as summer festivals, the tea ceremony and end-of-the-year celebrations. Furthermore, their annual album was entitled *Japonism* and included the song *furusato,* which had been used recurrently in NHK's content. During the promotional activities, the members expressed their purpose of representing Japan's magnificence and cultural richness through music, lyrics and performances. In August, NTV produced a special show to commemorate the seventieth anniversary of the atomic bombings and the end of the Asia-Pacific War: *Sakurai Shō & Ikegami Akira. The war which cannot be learned from textbooks.*[8] Broadcast during a Friday primetime slot, this was a hybrid between documentary and variety show, gradually changing the narrative's tone from educational to emotive and stressing the nobility of failure related to Japan's involvement and outcome in the war (Mandujano-Salazar 2016).

At this moment, Arashi was *the* national idol group unquestionably, and the discourses surrounding the members' representations were explicitly or implicitly accompanied by the weight of the national symbolism. In the following years, they continued participating in activities and projects of national interest and winning numerous awards. They repeatedly participated and hosted, as a group or as individuals, the *Kōhaku Uta Gassen* (NHK) and the *24-hour TV* (NTV), and continued hosting several variety shows throughout all major television networks. Their presence in Japanese media was pervasive, as well as the public recognition of their faces. Arashi won the Artist of the Year for the highest net sales in the music industry, corresponding to 2014, 2015, 2016, 2019 and 2020 (Recording Industry Association of Japan 2015, 2016, 2017, 2020, 2021).

Nevertheless, in January 2019, before their twentieth anniversary, the members of Arashi announced they would enter a hiatus of activities as a group beginning in 2021. During the press conference, they declared they wanted to dedicate the remaining months to expressing their gratitude to fans by performing numerous concerts and events (Nikkan Sports 2019a). Ohno gave the reason behind the hiatus; he stated that he felt tired and needed a break outside the media's eyes to find himself. Over the years, the five members repeatedly said their relationship was stronger and more profound than family, colleagues or friends. Thus, the remaining members explained that, although they were surprised by Ohno's decision, they understood and supported him. They also explained to the press and fans that, when discussing their options, continuing group activities without Ohno was quickly out of the table because the essence of Arashi was in each of the five members and their unity; therefore, they decided to pause as a group until he was ready to come back (Fukui 2019; Takahashi 2019). Being at the top of its popularity, the media and fans' reaction to the announcement only consolidated Arashi's role as the national idol. Japanese media corporations dedicated dozens of pages and hours of broadcasting time to repeat the press conference, analyse the history of the *kokuminteki aidoru*, praise the strong *kizuna* among them and interview people on the streets for their reactions.

It was during those last months that Arashi actively moved to reach younger Japanese and international fans. In response to the evident change in media consumption, mostly among young Japanese people migrating to streaming platforms to watch content, Arashi launched its YouTube channel and opened Instagram, Twitter and Facebook official accounts in October 2019. This was unthinkable for Johnny's idols before because the company was very strict on the rights over the images of its *tarento* and cautious about managing information. However, after Arashi, the launching of official social media accounts for the rest of the groups became a regular strategy intended to expand the acknowledgement of the Japanese idols beyond the domestic market by releasing short versions of the music videos and concerts, but also to strengthen the relationship of the idols with the Japanese fans by allowing a more direct and constant communication. Arashi's YouTube channel surpassed a million subscribers on the launching day and reached more than 3 million by the time the group initiated its hiatus (Hayashi 2019; Real Sound 2019; Yutura 2020). Likewise, aiming to reach international markets and expand its fan base, Arashi released English versions of numerous of its successful singles on YouTube, Spotify and other streaming platforms of international reach. Johnny's Jimusho also pursued collaboration with big names in the international music industry, like Bruno Mars, to write or produce some new singles for Arashi sung entirely in English (Johnny & Associates 2023a).

On 31 December 2019, Johnny's Jimusho globally released on Netflix *ARASHI's Diary Voyage,* a documentary series about the group. This documentary contains twenty-four episodes that follow the members from the press conference in which they announced the group's hiatus to the preparations and backstage of the last concert, *This is Arashi LIVE;* the last episode was released in February 2021 (Lu 2020; Netflix 2019; Sekiguchi 2021). The final concert on 31 December 2020 was how Arashi paused its group activities amid the sanitary restrictions due to the Covid-19 pandemic. The members and Johnny's Jimsho decided that given that the situation did not allow people to gather, their last performance should be a streaming concert offered to fans worldwide, in which they could express how much they valued the *kizuna* with the people who supported them over the years. Unlike regular Arashi concerts in which tickets were limited to fan club members, everyone could pay to watch the live streaming for this one. The strategy was very successful and allowed almost 100 million people all over the globe to connect live to the last performance of the group (Sekiguchi 2021).

Although these activities and productions were meant not only for the Japanese fans but for a global audience, the narratives accompanying them identified Arashi as the group representing Japan in all senses: as idols, entertainers, ambassadors of tourism and national values. Contrary to SMAP, Arashi was never involved in criminal offences, and the members kept a basically spotless social image. In fact, those last months reinforced the national relevance of Arashi in various highly symbolic events. The first was when the group became one of the few acts invited to participate in the celebrations of the enthronement of Emperor Naruhito, singing in front of the imperial couple (Kyodo 2019b). The second was their involvement in promoting the Olympic spirit for the Tokyo Olympics 2020, in which fans expected Arashi to perform. NHK had signed it to participate in its games broadcast, and the group had also planned to hold two massive concerts in the renewed National Stadium. On this aim, they released a song – *Kaito* – and recorded a promotional video in the venue. On 21 December 2019, Arashi was the leading performer in the opening event of the renovated stadium. Nevertheless, because the games were postponed until 2021 due to the Covid-19 pandemic, the group could only record a concert in the empty stadium and released the video in November 2020 for fans who paid the virtual ticket (Kyodo 2019a; Kyodo News 2020a).

Arashi continued breaking records in the music industry despite being on a hiatus. In 2021, the group won the Artist of the Year for the highest net sales in 2020; and, with the release of the videos of the last concerts, *ARAFES 2020 at NATIONAL STADIUM* and *This is ARASHI LIVE 2020.12.31,* Arashi had the highest sales of Music Videos in 2021 (Recording Industry Association of Japan 2021, 2022).

The analysis of the case of Arashi unveils the well-coordinated cooperation among the Japanese government, industry and media to build and promote a discourse about Japanese pride and identity in times of need and when a threat to national stability is perceived. Arashi is not the only *tarento* embedded with such narratives; female idols and athletes also play a role in disseminating these. However, the discursive focuses and their representations are diverse. Arashi and other Johnny's idols have as an ideological basis the promotion of national values and hegemonic masculinity traits, as will be discussed in the next chapter.[9] Moreover, Arashi and SMAP achieved a charismatic stance in Japan after a long process of maturation in front of the audience, transforming the members from teenage idols with fears and dreams into accomplished men who showed their commitment to society. As Aoyagi (2005: 35) said:

> In contemporary Japanese popular culture and mass society, successful idols […] are considered charismatic because they demonstrate the transformation from an ordinary young person to an extraordinary figure that influences the public. In Japan, charisma encompasses a person's abilities to face challenges, overcome struggles, and accomplish dreams against all odds. It also includes the person's ability to surpass the limits of tradition and attain a new meaning in life that can inspire other members of the society.

Although no statistical correlation can be established, the success of the pervasive banal nationalist campaign in which Arashi was a key participant promoting the recovery of national unity and pride during the 2000s and, particularly, after the Great Eastern Japan Earthquake, can be implied (see Table 6). The survey of Japanese Value Orientations of 2018 shows that in 2003 Japanese national pride and sentiment were at their lowest: 95.3 per cent of respondents felt proud of being Japanese, but only 35.8 per cent considered Japan to be a first-level country, only around half thought that Japanese society had better qualities than other nationalities and 66.1 per cent were willing to serve national interests; nonetheless, in 2018 all these criteria regain the levels of the 1970s, the peak of the *Nihonjinron* (Aramaki 2019).

During their January 2019 press conference and posterior interviews, the members of Arashi said that the decision to pause was carefully thought out and agreed upon by all members; they also revealed that they had talked about it with their managers and Johnny Kitagawa in February 2018 (Fukui 2019; Takahashi 2019). Hence, Kitagawa and the company's management personnel knew that the position of the national idol group would open. Therefore, the company had to begin promoting another one to keep the top position in the Japanese entertainment and media industries and maintain close ties with governmental cultural promotion projects. Consequently, many young units were being prepared; however, the heir apparent was King & Prince, a six-member group with a dynamic similar to Arashi and the last project Kitagawa promoted before dying.

Table 6 Nationalist values in Japan, 1973–2018.

Category	1973	1978	1983	1988	1993	1998	2003	2008	2013	2018
I feel good about having been born in Japan	90.5	92.6	95.6	95	96.5	95.3	95.3	95.5	97.3	97
Japan is a first-level country	41	46.9	56.8	50.2	49.2	37.5	35.8	39.3	54.4	51.9
Japanese people have extremely good qualities compared to other nationalities	60.3	64.8	70.6	61.5	57.1	51	51.2	56.7	67.5	64.8
I want to serve the national interests in some way	72.6	69	71.8	65.7	69	66	66.1	69.6	73.6	70.3

Source: Elaborated by the author with data from Aramaki (2019).

King & Prince, the heir apparent

In January 2018, after four years without launching any new group, Johnny's Jimusho announced the debut in May of King & Prince – formed by Hirano Sho, Nagase Ren, Takahashi Kaito, Kishi Yuta, Jinguji Yuta and Iwahashi Genki – under the record label Johnny's Universe, newly created by Universal Music (Johnny & Associates 2023a; Universal Music Japan n.d.). Two junior units with a few years of experience formed the group. According to the members' narratives in numerous interviews, Johnny Kitagawa repeatedly told them that he wanted them to be the first group of the company to aim for the global market. Allegedly, this was the reason for King & Prince to be signed under an international record company, instead of JStorm, as many of the current Johnny's groups (Web The Television 2018).

Although the six members were popular among Johnny's Jimusho teenager fans, Hirano was promoted as the group's centre to make it noticeable among a wider audience. As a junior, he starred in a youth-oriented late-night television series, *SHARK* (NTV). Then, a few weeks before the group's debut, the romantic movie *honey* premiered, having Hirano as the protagonist. He was also the male star in that spring's prime-time series *Hana Nochi Hare, Hanadan Next Season* (TBS), a new version derived from *Hana Yori Dango* (TBS) that had boosted Matsumoto and Arashi's popularity in the 2000s. The debut single of King & Prince, *Cinderella Girl,* was the theme song for this series. It sold over a half-million copies during the week of release, reaching more than 750,000 by the autumn, making the group's debut the most successful of the decade (Recording Industry Association of Japan 2018).

As part of the activities to promote the group's debut, the members appeared in numerous variety shows across the media. Essential in the campaign to broaden their recognition among audiences was their introduction in the prime-time shows *VS Arashi* (Fuji TV), *Arashi ni Shiyagare* (NTV) and *Sakurai Ariyoshi the Yakai* (TBS). In these, the narratives of Arashi's members explicitly stated the aim of getting people – particularly Arashi's fans – to recognize the younger group, its cohesion, talents, popularity among young people and the personalities of each member. Furthermore, the intertextuality and representation of the interactions between *sempai* (senior) and *kōhai* (junior) symbolically and discursively implied the acknowledgement of King & Prince as Arashi's successor. This kind of narrative and representation continued in the following months.

In October 2018, Johnny's Jimusho, under JStorm, in collaboration with Fuji TV, launched *RIDE ON TIME* (Fuji TV), a documentary series centred on the company's idols. The first four episodes were dedicated to the first months since the debut of King & Prince; the group was also the focus of the first three episodes of the second season. In these, the human and humble side of the members is shown, stressing their struggles, fears and weaknesses, as well as their motivations behind the effort they have to put in to keep up with demanding schedules and tasks to achieve the high-quality performances the fans watch (Fuji Television n.d.). Although the series is produced and broadcast on open television in Japan, it is also accessible globally in various languages through streaming services like Netflix, Prime and hulu (Vodzoo 2021). Furthermore, the episodes about King & Prince's second national tour stressed that Arashi's Matsumoto was one of the stage directors for the group's second national tour. In this way, not only Japanese fans who can access domestic variety shows received the implied message of Arashi supporting King & Prince, but also international fans.

During the first year of activities of the group, Hirano and the rest of the members starred in many teenage-oriented series and movies; as a result, their popularity increased, and their second single sold more than half a million copies. Nevertheless, in October 2018, Johnny's Jimusho announced that Iwabashi would retire from his activities for a time because he was suffering from panic attacks (Oricon News 2018). Similar to SMAP, when its members had troubles, the narrative of the members of King & Prince was to support him and keep a strong unity until he came back. The group was invited to perform in that year's *Kōhaku Uta Gassen* (NHK), which gave it visibility among the general audiences. However, Iwabashi never returned to the group and, in 2021, announced his retirement from the company to focus on his health. Thus, King & Prince developed as a quintet, like Arashi and SMAP.

In 2019, the same year that Arashi announced its imminent hiatus, King & Prince and its members began to be related to national labels in the media narratives across their numerous activities. They were usually praised for their looks and high-quality dancing, singing and performing skills, but also for their *kizuna* and their natural and distinctive personalities shown in interviews and variety shows, in which they were not afraid of making mistakes or looking silly, which reminded the essence of SMAP and Arashi. As a result, the group was awarded the title of GQ Men of the Year as pop icons; although some Arashi members had received the title individually, the group award was a first for Johnny's Jimusho (Model Press 2019). The same year, Hirano received the title of *kokuhōkyū ikemen,* or National treasure-level handsome man. This title is essentially a popularity award given biannually by the female-fashion magazine *ViVi* according to an open voting system among its readers who select the male *tarento* they consider the most attractive (Oricon News 2019b; Vivi 2020). In 2020, Nagase received the same title, and Takahashi reached the top five in 2022 (Vivi 2022).

The media dominance of King & Prince continued in 2020 and 2021 with the group's constant participation in music events of national interest, such as the *Kōhaku Uta Gassen* (NHK), *FNS Kayōsai* (Fuji TV) and the *Best Artist* (NTV). In those years, it also won the Gold Disc Award for its high-selling numbers in the categories of album and music video (Recording Industry Association of Japan 2021, 2022). In May 2021, to celebrate the group's third anniversary, King & Prince launched its official Twitter, Instagram and YouTube accounts; by December, its YouTube channel ranked third with the most subscribers in Japan (Real Sound 2021). Just a couple of months after the YouTube channel launch, the group presented the promotional video of the new single, *Namae Oshiete;* this song was produced by a Grammy-awarded American producer, Kenny Babyface Edmonds, and the lyrics were entirely in English. The members said that the song was recorded in 2019, in Los Angeles, as a first step in their intention to reach audiences beyond Japan.

Following the path of SMAP and Arashi of relating to a national-interest event with a social cause, in the summer of 2021, King & Prince was the leading personality for the *24-hour TV* (NTV) event, the first after the pandemic. Arashi's Sakurai announced it in one of his prime-time variety shows, *Ichiokusanzenmannin no Show Channel* (NTV). That year, the theme was 'Hope, the world will certainly change.' The members of King & Prince expressed their aim to motivate the nation after the pandemic and demonstrate that Japanese people could unite and find purpose after difficulties as long as they trust in their community. Through this participation, by the end of 2021, they had fulfilled their social role as leading personalities during a crisis. The Japanese media and fans began calling King & Prince the next *kokumiteki aidoru,* not only for their remarkable media presence and talents but primarily for the group's harmony, affability and differentiated personalities, which allowed the audience to empathize with each of the members (Bunshun Online 2022; Onishi 2021).

At the beginning of 2022, the group had its first family-oriented variety show, *King & Princeru* (NTV), which followed a very similar format to *Arashi ni shiyagare* (NTV), even reproducing the essence of the most popular sections of the show. On 23 May 2022, through YouTube Live, the members announced that they had received YouTube's recognition for reaching more than 1 million subscribers; they also told fans about the release of their fourth album, *Made in*, explaining that the title referred to 'Made in Japan' and 'Made in Johnny's' (King & Prince 2022). The central theme and promotional song – *ichiban* (meaning 'number one') – of the album and the group's fourth national tour relied heavily on traditional Japanese music elements and imagery – cherry blossoms, kimono – mixed with a contemporary style, very similar to Arashi's *Japonism*. Through this strategy, the members were symbolically reclaiming their stance not as the next but as the current national idols (Yoshioka 2022). During subsequent months, King & Prince's activities continued following the steps of Arashi. For instance, Takahashi became part of the regular *tarento* in a family-variety show about animals, *Sakagami Dōbutsu Ōkoku* (Fuji TV). Also, since 2021, *VS Arashi* (Fuji TV) became *VS Damashi* (Fuji TV), with Arashi's Aiba remaining as the leading host accompanied by other Johnny's idols; Kishi was one of them. Then, in 2022, Nagase was the main presenter of NTV's special musical show *Premium Music,* which in the previous editions had been hosted by Arashi's Sakurai. In the 2023 edition, Nagase repeated as the main host; King & Prince was the opening act and performed in collaboration with Disney characters, resembling Arashi's performances years before aimed to reach families.

However, on 4 November 2022, the members surprised their fans with a video released in the fan club media, in which Kishi, Jinguji and Hirano announced that they would retire from the group and Johnny's Jimusho after King & Prince's fifth anniversary. The same day, after that, they held a press conference in which they explained their reasons; the main one was that they did not feel confident about becoming international-level stars, as Kitagawa wanted, and that they held different opinions from the other two on which direction the group should take (Matsutani 2022; Sponichi Annex 2022). Hirano expressed his frustration for not being able to respond to Johnny's goal for them; Kishi and Jinguji expressed they did not want to remain as King & Prince if one of the members left. The five idols apologized profusely to fans and pledged to keep working hard until the last moment together to make them happy. Nagase and Takahashi declared they would continue working under Johnny's Jimusho under the same group's name.

All Japanese media covered this news as a serious one, just like when SMAP and Arashi announced their break and pause. After the press conference, the five members kept appearing together and released some singles, videos and an album before their separation. Almost since the group's debut, Hirano had explicitly and implicitly expressed in interviews that he felt the pressure of being the centre of King & Price and being expected to become a global idol. In one of the episodes of *RIDE ON TIME* (Fuji TV), he told the cameraman following him that, after important jobs and as a result of the accumulated stress, he usually suffered health issues. Regardless of this, he showed his compromise with the rest of the members and fans by continuing with various projects after the announcement. Kishi and Jinguji also kept working on the shows and series they had signed. Thus, although it is improbable that King & Prince as a duet can maintain the title, it provided Japanese fans, media and society with a national idol group until mid-2023. One of the essential symbolic characteristics of the *kokuminteki aidoru* label for Johnny's groups is the members' resilience and the *kizuna* among them to protect the collective, which resonates with discourses of traditional values.

Fans showed their support for King & Prince by buying the group's albums, singles and videos and subscribing to its fan club and social media so that it could achieve numerous records before the separation (KP Information 2023; Newage Repo n.d.; Oricon News 2023b, 2023c). Furthermore, in April 2023, just a month before the three members left the group, it was the most popular young group of Johnny's Jimusho according to the Talent Power Ranking's survey among men and women between ten and sixty-nine years old (Talent Power Ranking 2023b). Also, Hirano was voted the second most influential male *tarento* among Generation Z, only behind Arashi's Ninomiya (Talent Power Ranking 2023c).

After King & Prince, other groups debuted, and many other idols retired from the company; the stance of Johnny's Jimusho after Johnny died in 2019 and some scandals have affected the company's image, but not enough to disturb the media power of its idols. Snow Man, a group that debuted in 2020, is enjoying remarkable success in music sales and registered fans and has won the Artist of the Year in 2021 and 2022 (Recording Industry Association of Japan 2022, 2023b). Before its debut, the group had a long history as a junior unit; it was formed in 2009 by Takizawa Hideaki, who included the group in numerous of his plays and projects and continued supervising and producing the group when he retired as an idol (Ongaku Natalie 2023). Thus, fans are very aware of the group's qualities. However, with nine members, it seems to lack one of the characteristics of Johnny's national idols, namely, that general audiences – not only fans – can identify and relate to the personality of each one and that the group's *kizuna* can be evident to Japanese people. Nevertheless, it is probable that when Japan faces another crisis, this or another group derived from Johnny's Jimusho is pushed in media narratives to achieve the stance of the national idol.

Although the label can be used for diverse *tarento*, the national role is sustained by symbolic qualities required to support a national identity discourse that resonates beyond fans with the whole society and reminds Japanese people to unite in common aims to overcome the difficulties. On this goal, Johnny's idols seem more relevant than other *tarento* for their masculinity and personality features, which will be analysed in the next chapter.

Gendered ideologies and the support for male centrality in Japanese media

Japan has historically ranked very low in the World Economic Forum's Global Gender Gap Report, the lowest among developed countries. In 2023, Japan was 125 in a list of 146; ranking even lower than the previous year (World Economic Forum 2023). Thus, it is unsurprising that in Japanese television – the primary media for decades – there is also a gap in the social representations of women. According to a study on gender balance in Japanese television, women are less than 40 per cent of the people appearing; most are in their twenties, and less than 30 per cent speak (Aoki, Ootake and Ogasawara 2022). This representational gap nurtures the cyclical interaction between media and reality, reinforcing gender stereotypes and bias in the division of labour in real life.

Social representations build the common sense that dominates societies and provide people with stereotypes, values, norms, behaviours and emotional responses. Particularly during crises and conflicts, those representations support collective and personal identity construction, helping individuals define and evaluate themselves and the otherness (Moscovici 1986). In contemporary societies, the media are the leading producers of social representations that nurture the cultural background to promote ideal or transgressive models of social expectations. In this regard, the idols from Johnny's Jimusho are relevant in promoting social representations of ideal men. Furthermore, those who have achieved the status of national idols reinforce hegemonic models of masculinity that directly and indirectly impact social expectations on both men and women. Additionally, employing the sense of intimacy and affective connection they produce with the audience, they have enough social capital to promote dominant discourses regarding values and ideologies related to gender, family and work ethics, supporting their naturalization.

This chapter presents the results of textual analysis of Japanese media representations and narratives regarding Johnny's most iconic idols – those called national – and explores the main discursive lines that can be rebuilt from them in terms of gender and social expectations. These will be discussed in three parts: first, that related to a masculinity model based on physical attractiveness, strength and work ethics derived from their representation and supported by media narratives; second, the one related to a masculine role in social relationships based mainly on the personal narratives of the idols and the fictional roles they portray supported by the media's promotion, which nurture the imagination and ideals of the fans; and, finally, one which appears to contradict heteronormativity but, in fact, reinforce their masculine appeal with female fans.

The attractive masculinity of the national idols

As was explained in previous chapters, Johnny's idols have as first consumers young female audiences – attracted by a heterosexual desire towards the idols – and teenage boys – who see the idols as role models. As the idols mature in front of the Japanese audience, their manhood is reinforced by their representations and the narratives around them, turning themselves into models of masculinity. In her discussion about the masculinity construction of SMAP in the 1990s, Darling-Wolf (2004) stated that the gender symbolism of the members was hybrid in many senses: they were narratively presented as epitomes of male beauty, but they were also put in androgynous and cross-gender roles and imageries; and, they appeared to represent a more sensitive, less sexist type of Japanese man, challenging the stereotypes of the salaryman, but they were also shown in situations that perpetuated this model. In the representations and narratives surrounding Arashi, King & Prince and other groups that debuted and have been active in the twentieth-first century, I also find some androgynous and cross-gender representations. However, these are limited to fictional contexts and have an evident purpose, which is not to question the idols' masculinity; this will be analysed at the end of the chapter. In contrast, Johnny's idols are incessantly surrounded by a narrative that stresses their attractiveness, also manifested in their representations.

This attractiveness is undoubtedly defined in the context of manhood and expressed by the words *bidan* (beautiful man), *bidanshi* (beautiful young man), *bishōnen* (beautiful boy), *ikemen* (attractive man) or with the adjective *kakko-ii* (cool or stylish). The first three terms are used only for men who are socially considered as having beautiful physical – mostly facial – features. *Ikemen* is a term that refers to attractive men, and most times, such attractiveness involves not only physical attributes but also personality traits and the total impression that derives from their presence. On the other hand, *kakko-ii* implies the quality of being attractive or cool and stylish. However, this adjective is universal and can refer to males and females, animals or things; nevertheless, when used for humans, it acquires a masculine subtext that contrasts with *kawaii* (cute, adorable, pretty). Both adjectives are used to categorize physical attributes or behaviours and the impression that they give to others; *kawaii* describes features that are perceived as vulnerable or innocent and inspire the protective feelings of people and, as such, has a more feminine connotation; in contrast, *kakko-ii* stresses the perception of autonomy, strength or individuality, which gives it a masculine overtone.

The model of masculinity embodied by Johnny's idols relies on their physical strength and abilities, which are apparent even to the random audience, and are narratively reinforced to present them as ideal and desirable. Regardless of their age, they are consistently shown across media with stylish hair and fashion, pale and almost hairless skin and faces, a style described by Japanese media and audiences with the term *janīzu-kei*. Sometimes, they shave their heads, tan their skin or let their beards or moustaches grow for some role in a series or movie; these looks regularly get the attention of media and fans, who discuss it on social media, as it is considered out of routine.

Relevant examples of how they are discursively represented as attractive men and praised for their beauty without questioning or diminishing their manhood are the cases explained before in which numerous idols from Johnny's Jimusho have been awarded the titles of *kokuhōkyū ikemen* (National treasure-level handsome man) and *Man of the year* by the Japanese press based on the support of audiences. Likewise, magazine covers regularly present them with descriptions that, explicitly or implicitly, tell the readers that those features seen in them are attractive, desirable, cool and masculine. Numerous media launch periodic surveys in which people vote for the idols they find to represent these qualities (Rankingu! 2023; Trill 2023). In these, the narrative implicitly establishes that they are cool and attractive; it is only to find out who is the most.

Furthermore, their persistent portrayal of male protagonists in series, movies or stages supports their masculine representations. For instance, when they are the protagonists in romantic stories, their presence relates to narratives of feminine desire; when they are lead characters in historical stories portraying samurai or soldiers during the Pacific War, they are also explicitly related to past archetypes of masculinity. Also, in their interactions with other *tarento* in media, their status as attractive men in contrast with others is constantly stressed, either by explicitly being called as such or implicitly by the audience's reactions in the studio.

Besides their attractiveness, their physical abilities and strength are also constantly reinforced in their representations and narratives around them. The body type that dominates among Johnny's idols is slender but with defined muscles and is described as *hosomaccho*, in contrast with the *maccho* body type that refers to big muscular men. Although they are typically very lean, their physical strength is constantly emphasized in concerts in which they must sing, dance and run for hours and usually present performances that require extraordinary physical abilities. Similarly, they are routinely shown having to learn new things or develop new skills in record time. For example, between 1994 and 2017, the company organized numerous charity sporting festivals in which most of the idols participated and competed in two teams: East for those of the Kanto region and West for the idols of the Kansai area. People registered in the official fan clubs were the ones who could buy tickets, and the money was used to help victims of diverse national disasters (Oricon News 2016; Sponichi Annex 2004). In these events, the athletic abilities and the competing spirit of the idols, accompanied by a narrative that stressed their masculinity, were exalted for the pleasure of the fans.

Furthermore, during their variety shows it is very common to see them having their physical strength measured and athletic abilities put to the test and narratively build these features as an expression of their strong masculinity. A significant example is Tokio's *The Tesuwan Dash!* (NTV), which, since 1995, puts the idols on edge, making them survive in extreme situations, compete with top athletes and show their manly abilities to build houses or cultivate things. Another example is King & Prince and a regular segment called *Golden*

Rush that they had in a morning show, *Zip* (NTV), to promote the 2020 Tokyo Olympics. In this, they interviewed the Japanese athletes who would compete and had to experience some of their training and, in a few hours, show their progress; most times, they achieved significant improvement for someone who had never practised those sports, and the athletes praised them. Likewise, in their weekly variety show, *King & Princeru* (NTV), there is a segment in which the idols compete to find out who has the most extraordinary physical or athletic abilities. They have to recreate iconic action scenes of Tom Cruise, Keanu Reeves and Jackie Chan, perform the dance movements of Michael Jackson or test their strength against machines. In this segment, the masculine symbolism of the idols is strengthened by their demonstration of abilities similar to those of globally renowned male stars. Arashi also had those types of pieces in most of their variety shows, like *This is MJ* in *Arashi ni Shiyagare* (NTV), in which Matsumoto competed with other male *tarento,* many times another idol from the company, in a variety of situations aimed to show abilities that narratively were related to manhood, like parking a car in a small space. In this, the images were accompanied by titles or a voice saying that it was an *otoko to otoko no sumāto taiketsu,* meaning a smart competition between men. The manliness was further stressed in fictional situations where Matsumoto and the other male *tarento* had to learn fighting sequences in a very short time and act in a scene where they had to rescue a woman.

These representations and narratives also feed their hard-working images, which are another standard discursive lines around them stressed by the adjective stoic that usually is associated with their descriptions. In the backstage videos and documentaries of the diverse groups, the idols are shown sweating and physically struggling with the extenuating practices for their shows. All this hard work is accompanied by a narrative that stresses their intention to respond to the whole group's efforts and make fans happy. Thus, it is not an individualist struggle but one with a collective purpose, an idea that supports gender and national identity ideas.

Idols from Johnny's Jimusho are known for their strong work ethics, the hierarchical structure that resembles any other Japanese company, and their respectfulness towards other *tarento*. Throughout their careers, the idols share their experiences as trainees and interact with seniors, consistently demonstrating that they respect those with more experience or older than them, inside and outside the company. On the other hand, the shared anecdotes also reflect that they have a strong bond with idols younger or with less experience, and they mentor and protect them. Johnny's idols have to show their aptitude to be accepted in the company, and they should never diminish their effort and commitment. Once they are part of a group and debut, the members must devote themselves, assuming all the personal costs of hard schedules, lack of privacy and romantic relationships. Suppose someone breaks the company's strict rules or displays more interest in his personal goals than the group's; in that case, he is relegated from media and, typically, loses popularity and opportunities. Therefore, Johnny's idols generally exhibit an intense pride in belonging to their company, and their evident perfectionism and overworking resonate with ordinary Japanese people.

Finally, as detailed in the previous chapter, Johnny's idols are regularly involved in national projects or events to develop a broader audience beyond female fans or teenagers. Thus, their attitudes and social interactions are reminiscent of the archetypical Japanese men the salaryman represents in the vertical and group-oriented society depicted by the *Nihonjinron*. This model implies that respectable Japanese men must be competent and committed to their companies and nation by displaying continuous effort and loyalty (Vogel 1971).

Ideal romantic and social roles

Idols are meant to feed the fantasies of fans. Talking about the female idols, Aoyagi (2005: 218) stated that they offered their male fans what real-life women could not: 'forever accepting, obedient female personalities'. In the case of Johnny's idols, they also offer – male and female – fans what men in real life cannot, but in various roles: romantic partners, caring sons, grandsons or husbands, or always positive and cooperative colleagues or friends. These ideals are built mainly through the intertextuality of the personal narratives of the idols and their representations. In any case, their apparent availability is crucial.

One of the first ideal roles that Johnny's Jimusho promotes is that of a romantic partner for female fans. In this sense, there is an implicit rule in which the company only allows the idols to acknowledge a marriage publicly, which will be explained later. From their first appearances in media as teenage juniors until adulthood, the idols are frequently requested in magazines and variety shows to talk about how they would act on dates, anniversaries or marriage proposals, so female fans can imagine being on the receiving end. Because they are supposed to give answers to appeal to the fans and avoid releasing information about their real-life experience with women, it is evident to the audience that their answers are probably not concurrent with their actual thoughts and behaviours. However, this is not a problem because these interviews are a symbolic and narrative source for the fans to build their fantasies.

It is frequent for idols to pose or act in hypothetical romantic situations; when this happens, it is usually with another member or a female comedian. This is because Japanese female comedians are not symbolically related to beauty or sexual appeal, in contrast with actresses, female models and idols who are perceived as a threat among fans. In each group, a member plays the female role when needed to avoid problematical situations that can initiate or reinforce gossip. However, his representation is incongruent and meant to cause the audience to laugh. For example, in the case of Arashi, the role was usually played by Ohno, one of the shortest members, who has the least feminine attitude for Japanese hegemonic models. He usually expressed his preference for solitude, and his hobby was fishing, so he was always very tanned. In the case of King & Prince, the role was taken by Kishi, also one of the shortest, but whose physical strength, muscles and boyish presence are well known among fans.

In this sense, the variety shows of the groups also promote the participation of fans in the imaginary role of girlfriend in segments that exploit this along with specifically commercial aims. For instance, in Arashi's variety show *Himitsu no Arashi-chan* (TBS), there was a segment called *Mannequin Five,* in which the idols went to some of the newest or biggest shopping malls in Japan; there, they had to select an outfit that they would wear for a date. In this process, they were shown visiting the different stores and trying different brands of clothes. Then, the female fans were asked to vote and leave written comments on the outfits. In another episode, the idols whose outfits got the most and the least votes were revealed, along with some of the most interesting comments from fans. This was such a booming segment that, in five years, evolved to include the participation of male fans, and the show presented the results divided by the sex and age range of the respondents, consequently revealing the dominant taste of male and female audiences (Model Press 2013; PR Times 2011). In the variety *King & Princeru* (NTV), there was also a segment called *Couple's coordinate challenge,* in which the members went to fashion stores and selected their and their imaginary girlfriend's clothes for a date. They modelled their outfits with Kishi as a girlfriend, and a female *tarento* chose the one with the best fashion taste (Oricon News 2022a; The First Times 2022; Web The Television 2023). In these segments, the objective of the idols was not to be the lowest ranked because this was narratively related to not having a good taste for male fashion and not understanding the taste of female fans. Thus, while these sections serve as advertising, promoting shopping malls, brands and styles, the symbolic construction around the idols appeals to fans' desires. They also reinforce heteronormative patterns because male fans are also interpellated by inviting them to assume the role of boyfriends.

Another example of the idols actively acting in a romantic role for fans is the case of King & Prince's Jinguji. The group's fans – referred to as Tiara – began to call Jinguji *kokuminteki kareshi* (national boyfriend). He, the rest of the members and the media reproduce this label in a narrative that supports his representation of having the desirable qualities of a boyfriend, which are related to his consideration of the fan's requests (Real Sound 2018). One more is that of Sexy Zone's Nakajima Kento, who presents and promotes himself as someone who always has a prince-charming response to fans calling them Cinderella (Goo Ranking 2016). Furthermore, the role of the ideal romantic partner is reinforced by the entertainment media surveys in which audience select their desirable boyfriends, lovers or men they would like to date among the national *tarento* (Oricon News 2015, 2023a); and by variety and music shows reporting on the results of the surveys or the anecdotes of the idols with fans as if they were hard news.

In the case of female idols, one element that shortens their career is marriage or childbirth; symbolically, the very essence of a female idol is opposite to that of a wife or mother. Accordingly, the few female idols who maintain a media career must evolve into actresses, models or singers with a different discursive and media representation. During the twentieth century, the male idols produced by Johnny's Jimusho also had short careers because an idol was related to youth and singleness. However, during the twentieth-first century, particularly those who have achieved the status of national stars have transformed the symbolism of the male idols, demonstrating that they can be idols into adulthood and potentially assume private roles as husbands and fathers.

Although most of Johnny's idols are single, there have been more announcements of marriage, pregnancy of the wives, and the birth of children since the 2010s, when many have reached their late thirties and forties. In these cases, they send to the official fan club and media a written announcement stating the fact, and they ask fans for their continuing support, always promising that they will keep their effort to make them happy. Mainstream media covers this kind of news in a congratulatory tone, but they do not dig more into the personal details of the wives or children. Even after releasing a public statement about an idol marriage, the details are kept hidden as much as possible, avoiding the release of photographs or information that may offend the sensibility of fans. Mainstream media that collaborate officially with Johnny's Jimusho respects this by not giving space to gossip that may affect the image of availability of the idols. The idols are careful not to share details about their wives or married lives. However, they sporadically share anecdotes regarding their domestic shores or father roles, but interviewers do not deeply address this.

Most of the married idols have never talked about their partners. Only those married to known celebrities have revealed their wives' names. Nonetheless, they do not make public appearances together and rarely discuss them unless related to a mutual job. This aims to protect the appeal of the idols for the female fans, which depends on keeping the fantasy of their availability. Thus, when they share some details of their married life, these are not related to their wives; rather, they use a narrative similar to that of the idol's magazines, in which fans can position themselves in the partner's role.

In the case of the announcement of the birth of children, they usually appeal to fans' discretion. For example, considering the high popularity of Arashi, when Aiba announced that he would become a father, he asked fans not to try to get photographs of his pregnant wife for fear of her and the foetus's security (Cyzo Woman 2022). When the idols become fathers, they usually make alluring but vague comments about their children changing their life rhythm; sometimes, there is a narrative focus on their supposedly active involvement as caregivers (Chunichi Post 2022; Fukuda 2021; Nikkan Sports 2022, 2023). Interestingly, the acting roles the idols portray before their thirties rarely are of married men or fathers, but those of single men as romantic interests of female leads. After that, even in fictional roles that involve marriage, the narrative and representational focus tends to be on the elements of protector and provider and rarely on a romantic relationship with the wife.

Besides the ideal romantic partner, husband and father, the male idols' symbolism encourages building their images as sons, grandsons, brothers and even colleagues and friends in the audiences' minds. As discussed in the second chapter, one of the most common reasons for boys to enter the company relates to their mothers, grandmothers or sisters sending the application. Thus, from their earlier works, one of the reiterative narratives of Johnny's idols tends to stress the close affective relationship with them and share anecdotes but always keeping their relatives' identities hidden and referring to them only in their family roles. For example, it is common knowledge for fans of Arashi that Sakurai's mother is a teacher, his father is a bureaucrat and he acts like a caring older brother to his siblings. Also, Aiba and Ninomiya constantly talk about growing up close to their grandparents, and Ohno about how his mother bought his clothes well into adulthood. In the case of King & Prince, Hirano talked about living in Tokyo with his grandmother and becoming an idol to support his mother, who got sick when he was a teenager. This purportedly private information presented in a non-personal way allows audiences to position themselves in the role they prefer and according to the idols whose personality features are more appealing to them.

As Johnny's idols mature in front of the Japanese audience and take very diverse roles professionally and in fiction, even people who are not fans build an image of their personality traits and qualities and begin to consider them ideal models for diverse roles. For instance, in the case of the last decade's national idols Arashi and King and Prince, members Aiba, Kishi and Hirano are portrayed as very natural or spontaneous (*tennen*), kind, always optimistic and funny, similar to a *boke kyarā*.[1] They are represented and narratively built as very manly, with many innate abilities and talents, but also as men who make silly mistakes that make people around them laugh. Ohno and Takahashi are represented as having many artistic talents and taking things at their own pace, which in Japanese is called *maipēsu*.[2] Ninomiya is identified for his sharp mind, musical talent, somehow *otaku*[3] character, and his ability to make friends with older people. Matsumoto and Jinguji are the most committed and hard-working, with a broader vision of the situation around them. All of them are narratively represented as having an average family background and education, arguably making people feel comfortable and very familiar with them.

On the other hand, Sakurai and Nagase are portrayed as being raised in more privileged families. Sakurai, the son of a high-level bureaucrat, graduated from one of the most prestigious private universities in the country.[4] Nagase, the other son of a pilot, is also studying at a prestigious private university.[5] When Sakurai became a newscaster, he began to be narratively represented as an ambassador of his generation in serious national interest topics and a connection between different interests and social sectors. He repeatedly declared his aim of reaching the segments of the population not usually involved in the political, economic and social debates – meaning women and youth. He also took the popular culture to adult men, the core audience of news programmes.

As a result, in media surveys about ideal superiors or subordinates at workplaces, Johnny's national idols are expected to take some of the first places. For example, in recent years, Arashi's Sakurai, with his intellectual, serious and elite background, and Ninomiya, who is perceived as very sharp and capable, are seen as desirable superiors (Notani 2023; Takahashi 2022), while King & Prince's Hirano and Kishi, who always show their affability and persistent effort, have taken top places as ideal subordinates (Oricon News 2021, 2022b).

At the beginning of the century, Darling-Wolf (2004b: 361) described SMAP as representing in Japanese media 'a new generation of men conscious of the significant changes gender roles underwent in the latter part of the twentieth century'. Analysing the representations and narratives that involve twentieth-first-century male idols, I find that they certainly embody a model of Japanese men that has traditional and contemporary features: hardworking with interest in helping their nation and assuming heteronormative masculine roles, but also purportedly devoted to their families and more sensitive to women's needs. Nevertheless, the discourse remains hegemonically male, as this masculinity model is carefully built only with the idols' and the media narratives, selecting the audiences' voices that support it.

Beyond heteronormativity

Presently, people with gender identities and sexual preferences that challenge heteronormativity struggle for recognition and inclusion worldwide; a relevant factor is the underrepresentation and stereotypes of sexual diversities in media content. In Japan, about 40 per cent of people who identify outside heteronormativity have expressed having been harassed or attacked, and there have been suicides derived from the harassment they face (Kyodo News 2020b; Ryall 2019). However, it was not until the end of the nineteenth century that the government denormalized non-heterosexual practices. At that time, Japan entered a process of accelerated modernization and, aiming to be considered an equal by the European and American powers, the idea that non-heterosexual practices challenged biological reproduction and the reproduction of the economic model, they began to be presented as transgressors of order and common sense (Frühstück 2022; McLellan 2008; McLelland and Suganuma 2009).

Nonetheless, in the artistic field, Japan has a long history of popular expressions in which sexual and gender identities defy the contemporary notion of heteronormativity. For example, in kabuki theatre, only men act, and some actors specialize in impersonating women, the so-called *onnagata*. At the beginning of the twentieth century, its counterpart appeared in the form of the Takarazuka theatre, in which some actresses specialize in the impersonation of men and are known as *otokoyaku*. In both styles, the cross-dress actresses and actors adopt the gestures and adjust their voices to make their performance as feminine or masculine as possible, not as parodies, but as performances closer to the ideals than what cisgender men and women represent in their everyday lives (MacDuff 1996; Sakai 2020; Stickland 2004).

However, in mass media content, the representation of people outside heteronormativity has been typically related to homosexual males, transvestism and effeminateness in contexts of comedy or irony. Since the 1960s, the exception has been *yaoi* or *boy love* manga, a genre of comics in which women are highly active as creators and consumers; the characteristic of this is that it centres on male characters with androgynous aesthetics involved in romantic homosexual relationships (MacDuff 1996; McLellan 2008; Pagliassotti, Nagaike and McHarry 2013; Thorn 2004). This preference of some Japanese women for depictions of beautiful young men transcended into the real world and mainstream content in the form of the idols from Johnny's Jimusho, who play with transvestism and homoerotism to appeal to female fans, but at the same time do it amusingly, reaffirming their heterosexual masculinity.

As explained in the previous section, when there is a need to recreate a couple in the idols' variety shows, one of the group members, typically portrayed as very masculine, takes the female role. In these performances, contrary to kabuki's *onnagata*, they do not try to make their performances coherent; they overact some gestures and keep other masculine mannerisms to cause the audience to laugh. Perhaps, the best example is that of SMAP's Katori Shingo, who portrayed Shingo Mama, a female character that became very popular with children. Shingo Mama – with two ponytails and dressed in a dress and an apron – visited ordinary families and took the role of the mother for a few hours. Katori did house chores that stereotypically are considered for women in Japanese society, but his masculine corporality and overacting as a woman were incongruent and entertained the audience (Web Japan 2000).

Similarly, female fans celebrate the close interactions with a slight homoerotic mood between two or more idols in public appearances. These are so popular among fans that the term 'fan service' is used to describe them. In each group, there are at least a couple of members who, during variety shows or concerts, jokingly embrace, slightly kiss or show another kind of physical contact to cause the fans' excited reactions. For instance, in Arashi's case, it was common for Ninomiya to touch Ohno's glutes or for Ohno to kiss Matsumoto's cheek. These interactions inspire some fans, who transform them into *yaoi* style fanfics – written or graphic – that circulate in fan communities.

However, since the end of the 2010s, the portrayal of non-heteronormative roles has gone beyond comical sketches or short interactions. The idols from Johnny's Jimusho have begun to take leading roles in fictional stories that specifically deal with non-heteronormativity as the focal theme. In 2019, King & Prince's Nagase participated in *Ore no sukato doko itta* (NTV), a prime-time television series in which high school students – one of them Nagase – learned to appreciate and accept a transvestite gay professor after mocking and rejecting him. In 2020, Kanjani's Okura Tadayoshi starred in the movie *The Cornered Mouse Dreams of Cheese,* based on a *yaoi* manga; he played the role of a typical married salaryman confronted by an old friend who turned out to be gay and drives him to explore a homosexual relationship. The same year, Kis-my-ft2's Tamamori Yuta and Miyata Toshiya wrote, directed and acted in a short internet series, *Be Love,* a romantic story about a couple of men. Moreover, in 2021, Naniwa Danshi's Michieda Shunsuke and Snow Man's Meguro Ren starred in *Kieta Hatsukoi* (TV Asahi), another story based on a *yaoi* manga centred on two high-schoolers who develop romantic feelings for each other and end up dating.

Thus, although it seems that mainstream Japanese media are opening up to the representation of sexual diversity and exploring the psychological and social difficulties that people face when they are part of those diversities, they are doing so from a genre that has proven to be successful and emphasizes an eroticized representation of male homosexuality. Also, the non-heteronormative roles are portrayed by heterosexual men who are already attractive to women. As such, Johnny's idols are exploiting the appeal of these stories with female fans while they keep balancing these performances with their behaviour and public identification as heterosexual men, as has been presented in this chapter.

Hence, Johnny's Jimusho has developed a model of masculinity that is comprehensively pleasing. It appeals to women by presenting attractive men who can fill ideal roles for them, including by playing with homoerotic and cross-dressing representations. At the same time, it strengthens the Japanese hegemonic masculinity values by stressing the qualities of the idols as diligent, stoic and group-oriented men who make personal sacrifices for their groups, their company, their fans and, ultimately, their nation, which resonates with mature male audiences and traditionalist sectors. Furthermore, as some idols get married and have children while they continue in the company, the attractive masculinity model mixed with traditional salaryman values continues waving the flags of national identity and the centrality of men in Japanese society. Albeit these ideological elements of the national identity, pride and traditional masculinity archetype are embedded in the representations of the idols, the fact that they are the ones who carry the message makes it appear natural for Japanese audiences. Likewise, because the support of people is the reason behind the media power of the idols, it appears as if the Japanese society has selected them as ambassadors, concealing the faces of the company and media.

The identity-oriented performances of fans and the sacralizing of places and goods

Fans are the audience segments that most actively, intensely and effectively engage with the cultural objects of their desire to obtain meanings and pleasure, fantasizing and reworking them 'into a stylized matrix of practices and identities' (Williams 2004: 1–2). For fans, their practices are a form of identity construction; they shape their routines to build a physical and spiritual connection with their idols (Aoyagi and Kovacic 2021; Fiske 2005; Williams 2004). Fans are consumers whose practices are sustained in a set of beliefs and rules regarding their objects of admiration. Thus, these can be understood as religious; for them, there are sacred places and objects, as well as rituals to perform in and with them that can become ceremonies or habits (Fernández and Cachán-Cruz 2017; Jindra 1994; Löbert 2012). According to Belk, Wallendorg and Sherry (1989), consumption may be sacralized in different ways: ritual, pilgrimage, quintessence, collecting, external sanction, gift-giving and inheritance. In the case of the fans of Johnny's idols, various sacralization processes can be found in their practices. Then again, the idols create mediatized places through their representation, presence and association with specific stories, characters and spaces, and influence the meanings that fans give to them and impact how they perform in such contexts. As a result, these places become heterogeneous tourist spaces, in which 'transitional identities may be performed alongside the everyday enactions of residents, passers-by and workers' (Edensor 2001: 64). In contrast with non-fans who behave as expected regarding the original intention of a place, fans, for whom the places have become sacred after the presence of their idols, perform with actions, gestures and particular objects to symbolize and communicate their identity as fans of a specific idol or group. Also, there are experiences – like the attendance to a concert or event in which the idols will appear – that require items to be prepared and behaviours and practices to be followed in a ritualistic way.

This chapter will recover and analyse the sacralization of places and objects and the rituals that fans perform. It is based on information collected through ethnographic research over an accumulated time of twenty-two months between 2008 and 2019, in which I visited places related to the idols and attended concerts and events in Tokyo, Osaka, Sapporo and Fukuoka. Relying on participant observation, in-depth interviews and casual conversations with fans of Johnny's idols, particularly Arashi, I reconstruct crucial aspects of the idols' fan culture.

The sacred places and the regular rituals

For fans of Johnny's idols, there are regular rituals related to their identity as fans, as well as places and objects that become sacred through diverse processes. First, pilgrimage is found in fans' regular visits to certain places to get their favourite idols' latest photographs, goods or magazines. Some of these already have a sacred meaning for being sanctioned by Johnny's Jimusho, like Johnny's Store in Harajuku and Johnny's Family Club in Shibuya; and some are more profane, like the many stores selling unofficial goods (posters, keyholders, stamps) in Harajuku's Takeshita-dori. Located in the same area in Tokyo, it is common for fans to take a tour around all these places.

Johnny's store is open to everyone, but it has strict rules: it is forbidden to take photographs inside and only a certain number of visitors are allowed simultaneously; thus, particularly on weekends and holidays it is common to receive an entrance pass for a specific hour. The objects obtained there – printed pictures – are like sacred amulets, blessed by the company. They are not unique in a strict sense because each one has been printed thousands of times, but they are available for a limited time and cannot be found officially elsewhere; they even have a 'Johnny's & Associates' print in the behind of the photograph. Therefore, fans are motivated to visit the store recurrently to collect them, and their possession implies the ritual they performed to obtain them. There is a constant flow of fans of all ages – primarily female – all week long, but during weekends and holidays, there is typically a long line to enter.

Fans and their favourite idols are easy to identify because many carry eco-bags sold as official goods during the idols' concerts and events. Although the crowd is mainly female, it is common for fans to go in groups, accompanied by family members or romantic partners who are usually seen sitting outside the store waiting for the fans to do their shopping.

The other sacred place is Johnny's Family Club which, contrary to the store, allows entrance only with a reservation ticket to members of the idols' fan clubs (see Figure 1). Fans who want to enter must register on the official website, and there is a lottery. The selected ones get a ticket with the day and hour they can enter; this ticket is untransferable, and they must show identification; photographs inside are forbidden, and drunk people are rejected. This limited access makes a visit more valuable because only a few lucky fans who showed

Figure 1 Johnny's Family Club.
Source: Photograph taken by the author in September 2012.

their compliance with the process are allowed to be close to the hand-written messages of the idols, items they have worn or used during concerts and events, prizes they have won and had been in their hands, and they can directly deposit their messages to them in a letter-box. The strict rules also make the experience more similar to a visit to a sacred place (see Figure 2).

In contrast, the unofficial stores are profane and not exclusive to fans of Johnny's idols because they sell unauthorized goods related to many national and international celebrities. Nonetheless, these items allow fans to express their identity in more ways, like stickers on their phones and notebooks, keychains or posters to put on the walls of their rooms. Thus, although the stores are profane, the goods sold there are sacralized through quintessence by containing the idol's image.

A very relevant example of a sacred place by ritual, pilgrimage and quintessence is the case of *Keikarō*, the Chinese restaurant of the parents of Arashi's Aiba. The place – located in Chiba, about one and a half hours from

Figure 2 Sign of Arashi in the exhibition at the Johnny's Family Club in September 2012.
Source: Photograph taken by the author.

Tokyo – has a regular line of fans waiting to eat there and shows Arashi's posters and promotional images. Visiting this place is a regular ritual primarily for adult fans of Arashi, who have the financial resources to travel there. Their main objective is not to eat Chinese food but to interact directly with Aiba's mother, who cheerfully attends to customers, also, to be at a place directly related to their idol and feel that they are contributing to their success. Moreover, because the place is not controlled by Johnny's Jimusho, fans are free to take photographs inside as long as they do not disturb other customers; these are valuable for fans, but also for the business, as it obtains free advertising when they post them on social media.

Other places are profane but become sacred for a limited time through pilgrimage and ritual, like the temporary exhibitions from publicity campaigns, movies or series in which the idols participate. When these exhibitions take place, a long queue of mostly female fans can be seen from a distance; in many cases, the fans are so numerous that male security guards are placed around indicating where it is permitted to linger and take photographs and where it is not, so fans do not obstruct the commuters. Most fans go in pairs or larger groups. They photograph the exhibited images of the idols and also pose with those images. It is also common that they carry an *uchiwa*, a Japanese-style rigid hand fan made of paper or a carton that Japanese fans take to concerts and events to show who is their favourite member or to send the idols a message. Usually, fans carrying an *uchiwa* take photographs showing it along with the exhibited images.

For example, in the summer of 2008, as part of the promotional campaign for the *Hana Yori Dango Final* premiere, the broadcaster and producer TBS placed an exhibition outside its main building in Akasaka, Tokyo. It simulated one of the places shown in the story, surrounded by photographs from scenes of the movie (see Figure 3) and real-size cardboard images of the protagonists, including Arashi's Matsumoto. TBS also produced one of Arashi's regular variety shows of the time, *Himitsu no Arashi-chan*, and the TBS store nearby also had a cardboard with the image of Arashi. For days, female and male fans of diverse ages went to take photographs and sit around the exhibition, surrounded by images of Arashi and Matsumoto.

Fans do not limit themselves to their city when they want to pay their respects to their idols in sacred places. One prominent example is the case of

Figure 3 *Hana Yori Dango Final* exhibition and TBS Store.
Source: Photograph taken by the author in June 2008.

Arashi and Japan Airlines. Since 2010, when the group signed with the airline to be part of its campaigns, the members' image was printed on the exterior surface of some of the planes for a limited time. These planes, which also included the group's music as part of their basic repertoire, were called JAL Arashi JET and served domestic destinations (Japan Airlines 2010, 2011, 2012, 2015). Every time a new version of the JAL Arashi JET was launched, it was extensively covered by regular news and entertainment shows. Also, the airports served by them and the planes themselves became mediatized sacred places particularly attractive for Arashi fans who visited the airports only to see those planes and take photographs or to fly on them for the only reason of being related to their idols (see Figure 4).

In the summer of 2012, I visited Haneda Airpot one week after the third version of JAL Arashi JET was launched. At the aircraft viewing area, around the time the flight was scheduled to arrive from Fukuoka, about sixty people had their cameras ready. Most of them were adult women talking in couples or small groups and holding JAL advertising pamphlets featuring Arashi. Talking

Figure 4 JAL Arashi JET at Haneda Airport.
Source: Photograph taken by the author at Haneda Airport in 2012.

with some of them, I discovered that about half would travel on the *Arashi JET* that day. A recurrent comment about the reason for travelling to Fukuoka or Osaka – places served by the JET – was to experience being on that plane in a one-day trip. A couple of young adult women who identified themselves as Arashi fans since the group's debut said they had tried to get tickets for the first two versions of the JET, but they sold out quickly. For this third version, they had been able to buy tickets on a morning weekday flight to Osaka, so they had taken a day off their jobs. They would eat at some ramen place presented at one of Arashi's shows, do some shopping and go back the same night on another flight not served by the Arashi JET. They held the group's latest concert's eco-bags and hand towels. They explained that they carried them during Arashi tours, meaning when visiting places related to the idols' media activities (Mandujano-Salazar 2020).

   Another case presents when profane places and objects become permanently sacred by quintessence when an idol is shown in media visiting or consuming them; and, in addition, by the pilgrimage and ritual of fans. Regular transportation, street stands, restaurants, malls and objects – from food to clothes – can suddenly attract thousands of fans who want to be at, use or eat what their idols did. Particularly in the shows they host, there are segments focused on presenting the idols visiting diverse locations, going to famous shopping malls and tasting a wide variety of food from around the country. Of course, idols rarely invite the audience to visit or consume what they show explicitly. However, their visit to those places, experience with certain services or consumption of specific products turns them into sacred items and places for fans. This sacralization through the mediatization of places, products and services presented in the various shows where the idols appear also becomes part of a domestic tourism promotion.

I observed this dynamic on different occasions. For instance, in 2008, Yamashita Tomohisa – a very popular Johnny's idol – appeared in a morning show, *Hanamaru Market* (TBS), visiting Asakusa and eating snacks along the way. A few days later, the stands shown on television had photographs of him and signs made by the owners of those businesses indicating the products the idol ate. Likewise, in 2012, the show *Arashi ni Shiyagare* (NTV) broadcast a 1-hour episode in which the five members visited Mount Takao on the outskirts of Tokyo, mainly frequented by older people who like hiking. The episode showed many details of their tour, from riding a cable car to eating snacks at the different stages. Mediatizing the diverse spots along the road soon attracted young people and families. I visited a couple of months after the broadcasting and observed that the places where the members had been during the filming were marked with colourful tapes on the floor, and the snacks they ate were indicated with colourful notes. As expected, fans took photographs of those spots and ate those snacks. Many young women (see Figure 5) were walking with difficulty on the winding dirt roads, wearing clothes and shoes not designed for hiking. In addition, I interviewed a group of three high-schoolers who were wearing their uniform skirts and t-shirts from some Arashi concert. They said to have travelled from Shizuoka – about two hours by train – to be at the places they had seen their idols visit.

In 2013, *Arashi ni Shiyagare* (NTV) released a segment in which Arashi visited a place in Tokyo with internet reviews stating the delicious food and the owner's eccentricity. These restaurants had the characteristic of being small, inexpensive and family-owned, and received national-reaching advertising through this mediatization, adding a symbolism that was particularly meaningful for the fans. I visited numerous such restaurants and randomly talked with some customers, asking about their motivations for going there.

Figure 5 A food stand at Asakusa indicates the snack that the idol tried in the show.
Source: Photograph taken by the author in 2008.

I found that the presence of the idols was relevant even for non-fans; regular audiences expressed that, after watching the place and food, they wanted to try it. On the other hand, fans gave additional meaning to the places, food and experience; they expressed their desire to be in the same places that their idols had been, consume what they had consumed, and – almost as important – take photographs to share on social media. They were easily identified among other customers because they went in small groups, took numerous photographs at the exact places where the idols had been and displayed items related to the idols as part of their identity as fans. As a result, they felt part of a more extensive community of fans, and there was a symbolic value in being at the places sacralized by their idols.

The sacred rituals for meeting the idols

Perhaps the most important event for the fans of Johnny's idols to strengthen and display their identity is attending a concert. This involves many sacralizing processes, from external sanction, ritual and pilgrimage to collecting and quintessence. As explained in Chapter 2, tickets for the idols' concerts are sold only to members of the official fan clubs and, similar to the visit to the Family Club, not even this guarantees access; tickets are assigned by lottery among fans who applied and – although they sent their preferences – the venue, date and seats are randomly assigned. This process means that fans lucky enough to get tickets must adapt to those conditions to attend. If they do not want or can, they can pass on buying the tickets or buy them and then sell or exchange them, but this is a practice not officially allowed by Johnny's Jimusho, and, if discovered, fans can lose their membership or be suspended for other events. Thus, most fans adapt, making arrangements at work and home and travelling if needed because they know they may not get another chance to see their idols performing.

All concerts have a previous date and specific hours for buying official merchandise near the event venue. This merchandise is exclusive for each tour, and there are always eco-bags, *uchiwa* with the faces of the idols, and penlights with unique designs, which allow fans to be part of the show and interact with the idols during the concert. Other commonly available items are hand or neck towels, folders and posters, all with the tour title, so fans are motivated to buy them, regardless of having some of the previous events. Therefore, these items become sacred by the sanction of Johnny's Jimusho, pilgrimage and collection. Fans begin their concert ritual by going to buy these items.

Lines are long, and fans must stand for hours under the sun or rain to get them; they usually go in couples or groups, and it is common to see mothers and daughters going together. Female fans predominantly dominate this ritual stage, which is not exclusive to those who have tickets for the concert (see Figure 6). Numerous fans who did not get lucky in the lottery want to get the sacred items at least and feel part of the ritual. Thus, it is common to see fans standing or sitting around, holding papers in which they ask for a ticket. This practice is common, despite very few getting someone to sell them or give them an unused ticket; however, standing there is like a practice of faith that shows the fan's commitment to her idols.

Another part of the ritual is hand-making an *uchiwa*. Fans usually prepare at least one besides the official ones they bought. In the hand-made, they write a character of their favourite idol's name or messages and symbols, such as

Figure 6 Fans in the concert ritual for Arashi's *ARAFES*.
Source: Photograph taken by the author in September 2012.

asking idols to send a kiss or to make a gesture; if the idols happen to do some of these during the concert, the fan feels a close interaction.

Then, the day of the concert is entirely devoted to the idols. Long lines of fans carrying eco-bags filled with penlights and *uchiwa* are seen in the subways and trains leading to the venues. Security guards are placed from the main stations to the venue to direct the flow of people. The shopping malls, restaurants and convenience stores around get crowded with fans. The entrance to the venue is allowed only an hour or less before the beginning of the concert, so fans line up near the doors. The ambience is festive, with everyone sharing their passion for the idols; it is common to see groups of fans sitting, eating and talking as if they were camping. Amid the lucky and happy fans with tickets, there are hopeful ones expecting someone to provide them with one; however, if the doors open and they do not get an entrance, the fans without tickets remain outside the venue to listen or be part of the after-concert ritual. I talked to some of these fans on different occasions, and they shared their willingness to pay much more than the original value of the ticket. Some also said to have tried – without luck – to get the tickets online or at stores in Harajuku, regardless of knowing that they may get caught and denied entrance. Although Johnny's Jimusho officially forbids reselling, some people enter the fan clubs to get tickets and sell them overpriced. However, for highly valued concerts, like those of Arashi or King & Prince, only a few resale tickets are available and get quickly sold at exorbitant rates, sometimes exceeding the original price ten or more times (see Figure 7).[1]

Once in the venue, the ritual is very much determined. Fans are not allowed to take photographs; if caught doing it, they risk getting kicked out and banned from future events. Before the beginning of the show, once they locate their seats, many make a trip to the restroom because the concerts are around three hours long, and all minutes are valuable. The concert is the stage that is more diverse in sex and age of the participants, and there is relatively more male and children presence, mainly if it is a concert of groups like Arashi, SMAP or Tokio, which have a considerable appeal with wider audiences. Nevertheless, proof of the majority of female fans attending is that the venues always turn some of the male restrooms into female ones.

Once the stage lights turn off, fans turn on their penlights and begin chanting the group's name. Everyone respects their seats and stays there, standing or

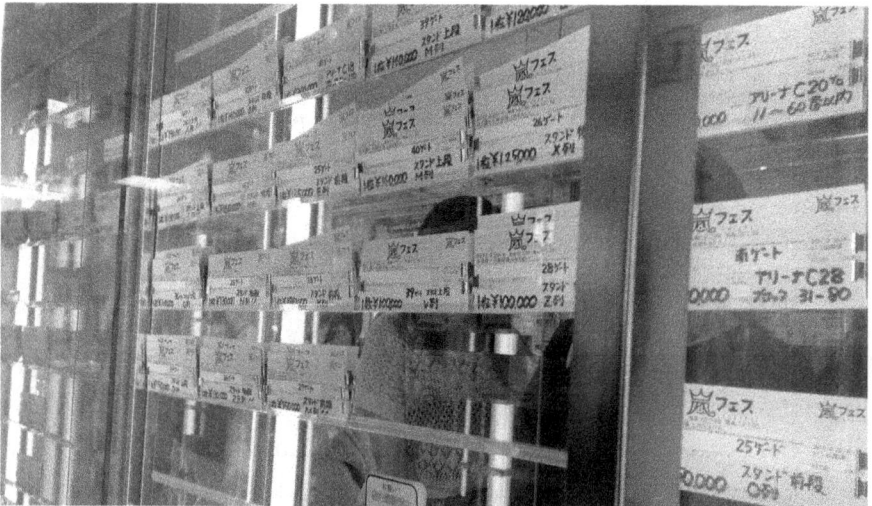

Figure 7 Resale tickets for Arashi's concert *ARAFES*.
Source: Photograph taken by the author in September 2012.

sitting according to the idols' indications. Fans must hold their *uchiwa* near their bodies and no higher than their shoulders to respect the visibility of other fans. If the idols get near a sector of fans, they may extend their arms carefully so as not to affect others or touch the idols; this is for the safety of everyone. During the shows, there is always a recess in which the idols stop dancing and singing and instead talk among themselves and with the fans, as a kind of small talk show. During this, fans sit and listen; they only react to the idols' comments or questions. The first time I attended an Arashi concert, in 2008, I was amazed by how more than 50,000 passionate fans could keep control of their emotions and perform as the company and the idols asked. On other occasions, when talking with fans about this, they explained that other fans reprimand those who act against the rules.

After the show, everyone gets out in order. Some fans stay near the road to glimpse the idols' transportation passing by, but most go back home or to their hotels. Because most concerts are on weekends two days in a row, many fans, particularly those that travel from other cities, try to get tickets for both days and, if they get them, they repeat the ritual the next day. According to the comments of some of these fans, this is very valuable because, although the show is the same, the talking section is different. Idols do not usually repeat conversations; these are mostly spontaneous and related to the anecdotes of those days, so this is valuable information that only the lucky ones attending that day can have first-hand. In addition, fans frequently share detailed reviews of each concert on social media and fans' communities, so those not attending can get the information indirectly. By sharing this, the ritual ends. As can be perceived, the concert ritual involves a high investment of time, effort and economic resources, and places, items and experiences are sacralized by many processes.

Another ritual for meeting the idols is attending the recording of their variety shows or shows and special events in which they appear. These occasions are more limited than attending concerts. Although every show has its process for selecting a studio audience, there is always a limited number of places – around twenty – and a range of ages according to the type of show. Also, for the variety shows of the idols, the recording is for two or three episodes, so attendees must clear their schedule for most of the day. Nevertheless, those lucky enough to secure a place rarely miss the chance to be closer to their idols and get to known conversations, gestures and anecdotes that will not appear on television.

Selected fans put special effort into selecting their outfits, hair and makeup because they will be in front of the idols for hours. They must be at the studio at a specific hour. As expected, studio audiences are forbidden to use their phones, record anything or talk during the recording. Idols enter the studio and welcome the audience before the recording starts. The most crucial role of studio audiences is to provide vocal reactions, so they must be attentive and respond accordingly to what is expected. Sometimes, there is an interaction between idols and the audience. When the recording stops, idols tend to make small talk with the audience, which are valuable moments for fans. At the end of the recording, the idols thank the audience for their time and support and leave the stage. Audiences must leave when the staff indicates it.

When interviewed about these experiences, fans who have attended as studio audiences concurred that they are willing to lose days of work and income if they can be near the idols. Fans expressed that on these occasions, more than at concerts, they exchange glances with them and sometimes get close enough to catch a breath of their cologne. Thus, this experience becomes the closest to a religious one.

The devotion of fans

Fans also perform in other ways to show their devotion to the idols and, in doing so, reinforce their group identity. One of the main activities fans of Johnny's idols constantly do is to create webpages, blogs and social media accounts dedicated to the idols they follow. On these platforms, they congregate and share official and unofficial information; some are essentially encyclopaedias that present every detail of the groups and the members. Most of the information is processed by the fans from the official channels – fan club accounts, newsletters, concerts, events and interviews in all media – but some also share the information that circulates in the media not aligned with Johnny's Jimusho, which tends to be gossip about romantic liaisons. Because of the restrictive policies of Johnny's Jimusho, these online platforms allow fans not living in Japan to participate and feel part of the fan community.

Although language can be a barrier, non-Japanese fans who live in Japan or speak Japanese translate much of this and other media information and share it in other languages, creating a bridge that helps propagate the adoration for the idols.

The power of fans and these virtual communities is particularly perceived when they act together to demonstrate their adoration for the idols, having a significant economic impact on the company. One recent and prominent example is the case of Tiara – the fans of King & Prince. On 4 November 2022, the group announced that three of its members – including the most popular, Hirano – would leave the group and Johnny's Jimusho after their fifth anniversary in May 2023. The fans rushed to buy the single released just five days later – *Tsukiyomi/Irodori* – to prove their unchanged love, turning it into the best-selling single of the year and breaking the record of a million copies (Oricon News 2022c). Still, they wanted more positive attention on their idols and called on social media for Tiara around the globe to break the one hundred million views of the *Tsukiyomi* promotional video on YouTube; they reached that mark in March 2023, something that all entertainment shows in Japan covered in their news section (The First Times 2023).

Furthermore, to send a message of their union as fans and support to the idols, in April, they began a movement in social media with the hashtags #oidera and #shindereragāruwomirionhe calling all Tiara to buy the debut single of the group, *Cinderella Girl,* to break the record of a million copies sold before the three members left the group. Almost five years after its release, the single went back to the top-selling list and, in mid-May, the single reached a million sales in the Billboard Japan Ranking (Nippon Terebi News 2023; Real Sound 2023). The fans also inundated social media with analysis about the future of the quitting members and their rage towards the company's management for not stopping them and retiring their images from most media before their official date of leaving; on the other hand, they praised the companies that kept their images, made some kind of tribute to the group, and invited Tiara to take photographs with their marketing posters containing the five members, like Honda, the magazine *Potato* and others (Entame 2023; Geinō Dasshu 2023; Sanae Toriko 2023; Shūkan Josei Prime 2023b).

Aware of this behaviour, Johnny's Jimusho profited from fans' devotion. For the last months of the group as a quintet, King & Prince released one single, one album and two concerts on DVD and Blu-Ray (Johnny & Associates 2023a). The single sold more than a million copies in the first week of its release (Billboard Japan 2023); the two concerts broke the half-million record consecutively, a mark only imposed by Arashi before (Oricon News 2023d), and the album broke the million mark in two days (CD Journal 2023; Flash 2023).

Then again, not only the fans' devotion but also their rivalries are the foundation of Johnny's Jimusho business model. Rivalries are common among fans of different popular groups of similar ages; in recent years, fans of King & Prince and Snow Man have been competing to make their group the most popular, recognized and with the most records. This rivalry among them has pushed the selling numbers and the registered members for both groups' fan clubs in Johnny's Jimusho (KP Information 2023; Newage Repo n.d.).

Additionally, fans defend their idols, even from others in the same company. For example, when Sexy Zone's Kikuchi made a comment criticizing artists who were focused on breaking into the American market, Tiara thought this was a critique of the three members leaving King & Prince, and the fans responded angrily on social media (Tokyo Sports 2023). Likewise, if fans perceive that the company is mistreating their idols, they respond. After the death of Johnny, his niece Fujishima Julie Keiko assumed the company's presidency. On the other hand, Takizawa Hideaki, a protégée of Johnny since his incorporation as a junior in 1995 who had retired as an idol to become part of the company's producers in 2018, became vice president. The fact that a former and very popular idol, known for getting along with seniors and juniors, became vice president gave fans the hope that things inside the company would keep running smoothly for the idols. Nevertheless, a series of disbandments and retirements from the company have been shaking the fans and Japanese media since then.

In September 2019, Kanjani's Nishikido announced he would leave the company at the end of the month (Oricon News 2019a). Then, in June 2020, the company terminated the contract of NEWS' Tegoshi Yuya, causing fans' rage (Sakashita 2020). In July, Tokio's Nagase Tomoya said that, after twenty-six years, he would leave the company (Kyodo 2020). In November, Yamashita Tomohisa, one of the most popular idols and very close to Takizawa, also announced his retirement from Johnny's Jimusho (TV Asahi 2020). The parting of idols continued in 2021; V6 disbanded, and one of its members – Morita Go – left the company (Ronald 2021). Later, in November 2022, Takizawa announced his resignation from Johnny's Jimusho, only a few days before the announcement of King & Prince about three members' withdrawal (Josei Jishin Henshubu 2023). In December, a popular junior unit produced by Takizawa – IMPACTors – announced that all members would abandon the company (Smart Flash 2022). During 2023, the trend continued with V6's Miyake Ken resigning in May and Kis-My-Ft2's Kitayama Hiromitsu in August (Oricon News 2023e; The Yomiuri Shimbun 2023).

When Johnny was alive, there was never such a rush out of popular idols. A few of them left the company, but most retired after a long time outside the media or for some misconduct that Johnny's Jimusho considered inappropriate for the image of its groups. At least until writing this book and despite the scandal that will be explained below, none of the idols who quit recently declared a bad thing about the company. On the contrary, they exposed to fans and the media their decision as personal and related to their desire to pursue other interests. Nonetheless, fans have reacted and questioned if the remaining idols should stay at Johnny's Jimusho and blame Fujishimas's cruel and discriminatory treatment for the debacle that has been called *yamejani* – or the 'quitting Johnny's' (Brasor 2019; Geinō Dasshu 2023; Josei Jishin Henshubu 2023; Matsutani 2022; Ota 2020; Trend Magazine 50 2023).

Another change from the new administration, which has caused fans' adverse reactions, is a new juniors system established in April 2023. By this, those who reached the age of twenty-two without debuting will have their contract terminated. The company argued that this system aims to give the trainees freedom to change professional paths because, in the past, many juniors had remained in the company well into their late twenties, hoping to debut and never did. In Japan, professional development is expected to begin around twenty-two years old, the average age for finishing university. Therefore, Johnny's Jimusho argues that the age limit would allow juniors to reinsert into regular society through other careers (Shūkan Josei PRIME 2023a).

On 21 March 2023, Takizawa announced on his Twitter account the establishment of a new entertainment company, TOBE (Takizawa 2023). On its official webpage, Takizawa sent a message to fans and aspiring idols: through this company, he aims to build a new form of entertainment based on the union of fans and *tarento* in a less restrictive way (TOBE 2023a). Fans of the idols who quit immediately began taking to social media their hope for them going to this company, expressing that they will follow them. Numerous Tiara even said they would like the remaining two members of King & Prince to quit Johnny's Jimusho and reunite with the other three under Takizawa's production. While writing this book, Miyake, Hirano and Jinguji signed with this company; IMPACTors, under the new name IMP., signed and made their debut with a digital single (TOBE 2023b).

It is evident that fans are devoted to the idols, not the company, and Johnny Kitagawa understood this. Such is the explanation behind his empire: the idols and fans' relationship; and the identities and ideologies portrayed by the idols that are translated into symbolic power. This strong bond is perceived even whilst the company is facing a backlash from Japanese media and society due to the exposure of Kitagawa's sexual abuse to juniors over the years. Fans, while confused about the implications for their idols and regardless of this meaning to support profits for Johnny's Jimusho, continue to buy the groups' products and go to their shows.

Beyond the scandal of sexual abuse inside Johnny's Jimusho: The future of the male idol industry in Japan

For decades, there was a rumour that circulated among Japanese society and fans of Johnny's idols around the globe. As mentioned in Chapter 1, in 1999, a Japanese investigative weekly magazine – *Shūkan Bunshun* – released a series of reports in which a dozen men who had been juniors at Johnny's Jimusho in the 1980s revealed that Johnny Kitagawa had approached them sexually while they were very young teenagers. Kitagawa sued the magazine for defamation and won, which was covered by mainstream media. In contrast, in 2004, when the magazine appealed and, after listening to the declarations of the former juniors, the Tokyo High Court ruled that most of the claims in the articles were credible, the case was not reported by major media corporations (Bunshun Online 2023; Chon 2023; Cyzo Woman Henshubu 2023; Joho Station Tokuneta 2019; Nakamura 2022; Shūkan Bunshun Henshubu 2023; Yano 2016).

Johnny's Jimusho was able to keep it as gossip and this did not cause any societal reaction for almost two decades. Indeed, in practical terms, this was due to the company's power over mainstream media by controlling the rights over the access and image of the most popular idols in the country. However, in essence, it can also be attributed to the scarce social interest in the topic. The reasons for this are related to cultural and legal elements. First, throughout Japan's history, there are contexts of accepted – even respected – male homosexual power relations. For instance, in the Heian period (794–1185) there were numerous accounts of *chigo* – young boys in Buddhist temples – involved in homosexual relationships with older priests; and, during the Edo period (1603–1867), the *wakashūdo* was a relationship involving an older man and a young boy that was regarded as part of young men's path to acquire the male values of the time (Jackson 1989, 2016, 2019; Pflugfelder 2012; Schmidt-Hori 2009; Stoneman 2009). Hence, even if contemporary Japan has other values and these practices are not accepted anymore, the social perception of the issue was that it had the tone of an old legend.

Furthermore, Japan is a country in which legality is highly valued. Japanese people tend to emphasize rules and laws to interpret something as acceptable or not. In this regard, until 2017, the definition of rape in the Penal Code of Japan was something specifically limited to females as possible victims; moreover, it had to involve the explicit use of physical violence and intimidation (UN Women 2023). Even after 2017, with the inclusion of men as potential victims, the elements of forceful assault and thirteen as the age of sexual consent remained. The notion of sexual consent in this context limited what could be considered assault if no violence or explicit intimidation was involved (Mainichi Japan 2022; Nakata Atsuhiko 2023). Hence, because the case of the rumours about Kitagawa lacked those forceful elements and involved men who were over the legal age of sexual consent, the issue was not deemed illegal.

Therefore, until very recently, there was barely a mention of the allegations in the Japanese fans' social media accounts. Instead, what fans talked about and emphasized over the years were the anecdotes that the idols recurrently shared in the media. Every debuted idol had publicly shared, with apparent respect and affection, experiences of his time as junior and funny and endearing anecdotes about Johnny Kitagawa (Yamamoto 2022). Even the youngest who spent less time with Kitagawa – such as the members of King & Prince, Snow Man or SixTONES – expressed their gratitude to Johnny after his death. Furthermore, over the years, there were idols whose parents were known to have respectable positions and economic resources, like bureaucrats, famous artists and older idols.[1] Thus, society and fans took this as evidence that Kitagawa could not have been hurting the juniors without anybody doing something to stop him.

Accordingly, when Kitagawa died in July 2019, all the idols of the company went to his funeral, and the media followed it as a significant national event. Also, during a press conference, then-Cabinet Secretary Nogami Kotaro recognized Kitagawa's vast contribution to the national entertainment industry. Likewise, fans began a trend on Twitter with the hashtag #ThankyouMrJohnny, a fact that was even reported in Chinese media (CGTN 2019; Nikkan Sports 2019b; Sansupo 2019; Shūkan Josei PRIME 2019; Sponichi Annex 2019).

Nonetheless, when non-Asian media informed about the death of the Japanese entertainment mogul, they also stressed the control he held within the Japanese mainstream media (Koh 2019; Oi 2019). Besides, the BBC even mentioned the rumour of his abuse of children (Schilling 2019); none of which was news to fans, so it did not cause any reaction from them.

However, at the beginning of March 2023, in the context of Japan's Cabinet approval of a bill to raise the age of sexual consent to sixteen and to recognize violation without physical coercion (Kyodo 2023; Ng 2023), and almost four years after the death of Kitagawa, the BBC released a documentary about the sexual abuse allegations against him. It soon attracted attention from international media and, inside Japan, from gossip and social media.

The documentary presented the reporter Mobeen Azhar, in Tokyo, trying to investigate the claims but having difficulties because he did not get any concrete answer from Johnny's Jimusho, mainstream media, music corporations or the police. The Japanese people interviewed on the streets responded that they had heard the rumour. Yet, they said not to be interested in getting it explored; on the contrary, some interviewees were shown declaring that Johnny was like a god. The reporter presented three men – two of around fifty years old and the other around thirty – who declared to have been sexually touched by Kitagawa when they were juniors in their teens, but they were reluctant to call it abuse, and they reaffirmed their affection for Johnny. Another interview showed a twenty-three-year-old former junior who said he heard the rumours but never experienced a sexual advancement from Johnny; this man also stated that he would have accepted it if that had secured him to become famous (Azhar 2023; BBC News Japan 2023).

Azhar recurrently and strongly expressed his surprise at the Japanese society and institutions for their silence and not wanting to engage in the conversation about such problematic allegations. He also stressed his interpretation about the alleged survivors being under a trauma bond with Kitagawa, which – he argued – must be the reason for them not accepting it was abuse (Azhar 2023; The Foreign Correspondents' Club of Japan 2023a).

The allegations were unquestionably upsetting and they appeared in the context of an ongoing discussion inside Japanese society about the need for a full revision of the laws regarding sexual abuse. The investigation presented by the BBC did not provide compelling evidence of Kitagawa's systemically hurting hundreds of children – including the debuted idols – as the narrative implied. On the other hand, it did confirm two situations: the power that Johnny's Jimusho had inside Japan, as proved by all mainstream media, including the public broadcaster NHK, rejecting to give any declarations to the BBC's reporters; and, also, the BBC's ethnocentrism and unawareness about Japanese culture and the social and ideological role of Johnny's idols in the country.

In the documentary, Azhar entered an unofficial idol store and, looking at dozens of photographs of the members of Arashi and Hey! Say! JUMP, he said:

> It is such a specific type. I mean, they look young. None of them has a beard. You know, there is a particular hairstyle, a particular face type, there's a kind of innocence and a boyishness, […], they know what the brand is, that's what they are selling. They are all kinds of reflections of one image. There is so little differentiation between these guys, is almost as if the boys themselves are not the point; is the vision, is kind of what you're buying into, is the brand, and these guys all are just reflections of that.
>
> (Azhar 2023: 25:42–26:24 min)

He said this without understanding that for the Japanese audiences and, particularly for fans, Johnny's idols are much more than their images. Indeed, there is a brand and a physical style that is well-regarded by fans, but the idols are not merely reflections of boyishness or interchangeable faces; they are valued for their very well-defined personalities, as well as for the ideologies and identities they represent. Moreover, in this sense, the allegations regarding Kitagawa did not impact directly the role of idols in Japanese society or what they symbolize; but the scandal derived from them potentially did.

Stressing the power relations between nations, Said (1985, 2003) problematized that Europe and the United States have historically imposed their interpretations and rhetoric over other societies according to their particular interests and projects. In his original work, one of the many elements he analysed was how, since centuries ago, European – fictional, autobiographic and academic – accounts about Asia and Africa built the *Orient* as a set of imagined references to exoticism, perverse morality and dangerous sexual practices. In 2023, one of the most influential European media corporations, the BBC, reproduced these images and discourses around the world, opening

Pandora's box about a very delicate issue to be discussed and resolved within Japanese society. After six decades of rumours without consequences, the foreign attention caused public reactions inside Japan and *Shūkan Bunshun* released the past interviews along with new testimony from a younger ex-junior, Okamoto Kauan, who talked about Kitagawa's sexual advances with him in front of The Foreign Correspondents' Club of Japan (Bengoshi Dot Com News 2023; Okamoto 2023; Shūkan Bunshun Henshūbu 2023; The Foreign Correspondents' Club of Japan 2023b).

This pressured a public acknowledgement from Johnny's Jimusho. On 14 May 2023, Fujishima Julie Keiko, as president of the company, broke the silence and released a video issuing a public apology to the alleged victims, people related to the company and fans. The video was accompanied by a written interview in which Fujishima explained that, after the BBC documentary, the company was performing an investigation and would apply measures to prevent such practices (Benoza and Takahara 2023; Johnny & Associates 2023b). As an immediate reaction and for the first time, Japanese mainstream media, including the NHK, covered the news about the video and mentioned the case of Okamoto and the BBC documentary (Netorabo 2023). Then, a few other ex-juniors abused by Kitagawa spoke out and went in front of Japan's legislators to appeal for changes in the law to better protect children (ANNnews 2023).

The narrative that the BBC instigated along with the new testimonies, some of which mentioned popular and national idols, places them either as probable victims or as accomplices for remaining silent. Whether they were abused or not, or whether they knew about the abuse of others or not, the fact is that they were subject to power relations inside the company, so they were also in a weak position and now they were suddenly being outed by foreign media. In this sense, not only debuted idols but also former juniors spoke and denied they were abused or knew something concrete beyond the rumours (Mori Channel 2023; TBS News Dig 2023). On the other hand, fans questioned if the new accusers were using the names of popular idols to gain fame without caring about how the scandal affected their image and reputation (Takō 2023).

On 7 September 2023, after a third-party investigative body determined through interviews with former juniors and staff that Kitagawa had sexually abused numerous boys inside the company over the years, Fujishima quit as president but remained the absolute shareholder. Higashiyama Noriyuki, the oldest active idol of Johnny's Jimusho took the role of President (Kaneko and Takahara 2023; Ueno and Dooley 2023; Yeung 2023). Because the silence of mainstream media had also been accused as part of the problem, all major television networks – many of which had Johnny's idols as announcers in their shows – covered the news and made the idols express their opinions on the issue (Matsutani 2023).

According to Nietzsche's famous phrase, there are no facts, only interpretations (Viscomi 2019). Following this premise, Foucault (1980) argued that what functions as the truth in a society results from the struggle of interpretations from social groups in that particular context. Furthermore, as Han (2017) expands, in contemporary societies, the paradigm of apparent freedom to choose – created by an infinite offer of products, images and information – effectively hides such struggle and the power structures behind the dominant interpretations and ideologies, making their naturalization more effective. In this sense, the giant media corporations, with their expansion throughout all entertainment and information niches, are the actors that can easily impose a regime of truth on society through recurrent narratives and representations across products, genres and technologies.

In Japan, Johnny's idols had been prevalent image commodities that were generally interpreted the same way by Japanese society and fans because the producer company, mainstream media, and political and economic powers had a consensus on the values and ideologies to embed in their representations and narratives. As argued throughout this book, the idols produced by Johnny's Jimusho, particularly since the turn of the century, have had the role of promoting national identity and traditional masculinity values: social harmony, resilience, sacrifice, pride and love for Japan, physical strength and abilities, devotion to one's group/corporation/nation, solid emotional bonds inside the groups, respect towards seniors, care of juniors, care for parents and family members and desire for the reproduction of the family structure.

Boorstin (1992) argued that celebrity worship and hero worship are not the same because heroes were symbols of the ideals and morality of their time. In contrast, celebrities are created by gossip and public opinion and can be easily substituted. In the case analysed here, the worship of Johnny's idols is in the middle. They are celebrity-like commodities produced carefully with specific characteristics and embedded with dominant ideologies. Nonetheless, these symbolic features represented for decades the morality and ideals of contemporary Japanese society negotiated between the producer powers and the audiences that sustain them.

As demonstrated, although the fans of Johnny's idols include people of any sex, unrelated to their gender identities, those actively involved in sacralization rituals are predominantly adult and teenage women. Their rituals and investment of all kinds of resources involve a profound knowledge and comprehension of the context of the idols' production. Fans are not ignorant nor naive; they are aware of how Johnny's Jimusho profits from their behaviours and controls the information distributed by mainstream media by limiting the rights to use the images and names of its idols. Even so, they understand that it is the controlled and meticulously built system that has made and sustained them. Therefore, fans comply with the rules imposed by the company and accept the narratives propagated by mainstream media because they would not do something that may hurt the idols, even if that means giving the company more power and economic gains.

Consequently, Johnny's Jimusho became an economic and ideological powerhouse in Japan until recently, maintaining a monopoly on producing successful male icons that were more than entertainment celebrities; they were accepted as ambassadors of national values and masculinity ideals by large portions of society, and fans were willing to support this machinery as long as the idols were protected. However, it grew too strong and this hid problematic practices inside, which exploited and controlled – in different ways – young men in the process of their transformation into idols.

In this troublesome context and with the establishment of Takizawa's company TOBE, the hegemony of Johnny's Jimusho in Japanese media is uncertain. Perhaps, this will open the market for some competition that offers fans and society the same symbolic experiences and provides better practices for the benefit of the idols and fans. Also, the recent scandal possibly will help Japanese society to openly debate the need for a revision not only on the laws regarding sexual abuse but also on practices that have remained normalized.

Glossary

Amae An emotional dependence on superiors.

Bidan Beautiful man.

Bidanshi Beautiful young man.

Bishōnen Beautiful boy.

Boke-kyarā A funny or silly personality.

Giri Obligation towards someone.

Honne The expression of self-consciousness.

Honne-ni-semaru The practice in Japanese media to ask *tarento* for inside stories or their thoughts about some topic.

Hosomaccho Slender man that has defined muscles.

Ie Traditional Japanese household or its hierarchical structure.

Ikemen Handsome or attractive man.

Janīzu-kei The look or body and face type of Johnny's idols.

Jimusho Literally, office. In the context of the book, it refers to the management agencies of *tarento*.

Kakko-ii Cool or stylish.

Kareshi or kare Boyfriend.

Kizuna Social ties, bond or connection.

Kōhai Junior in hierarchical relationships.

Kokuminteki The quality of being considered representative of the nation.

-kun Suffix that is used after the name or surname of people with the same or lower status in the hierarchy. It is more common for male interlocutors but may be used for females in professional and academic contexts.

Maipēsu A type of personality in which the person does things his/her own pace.

Nihonjinron Japanese ideological or cultural nationalist movement popular during the 1970s and 1980s.

Omote The attitudes and expressions used by someone according to the circumstances they are facing.

On Indebtedness from one person to another.

Sekentei A sense of decency according to society's standards.

Sempai Senior in hierarchical relationships.

Sengyōshufu Full-time housewife.

Sugao or sunao Honest, truthful.

Tarento The general category to refer to Japanese media personas. It is used for singular, plural, masculine and feminine.

Tatemae The expression that is framed by social conventions.

Tennen A natural or spontaneous personality.

Tsukkomi A personality that likes to pick on people.

Ura The truthful mind of someone that is not shared in public.

Urabanashi Inside stories.

Notes

Chapter 1

1   The *Talent Power Ranking* is produced since 2008 by Architect Co. Ltd., a marketing company, which sells a detailed version to entities that need to decide on the best *tarento* to endorse their products. The general top ranking is found freely in entertainment magazines, websites, or referred to in television to let know the audiences who are the most powerful *tarento* and reinforce their status. This ranking is another of the elements in the intertextual construction of the *tarento*.

2   This concert has been held annually since 1951 by the public Nippon Hōsō Kyōkai (NHK), as part of the special shows for the celebrations of New Year. Currently, it is broadcasted live for four and a half hours, the last of each year. It is considered as one of the most important media events, typically achieving the highest annual ratings. The performing artists are chosen by a committee of the NHK and are announced in a ceremony some weeks before. The selection considers the tastes of the national audience, and for such reason, all media – including private corporations – report on the event. The show's format is a musical competition between a red team and a white team. The red is formed by female artists or groups with female leading singers, and the white is formed by male artists or groups. Another important selection is the masters of ceremonies, who also act as captains of each team, and the roles, also one female and one male, are awarded to *tarento* who were nationally relevant that year. After artists' performances, the public and a committee of other invited *tarento* or public personalities vote to select the winning team. Finally, the flag of victory is presented to the master of ceremonies representing the winning team and the show ends at 11.45 pm (NHK n.d.c).

Chapter 2

1   For an analysis of the marketing strategies of contemporary female idols, like those produced by Akimoto, see Galbraith and Karlin (2012) and Galbraith (2012, 2018).

2 During the analysis period, there were only reports about a couple of incidents in which someone threatened an idol during a stage, and they were quickly controlled without victims. The fact that only registered fans can get tickets allows the company to punish those who behave against the rules during the events, banning them for some time or permanently, according to the seriousness of the fault.

3 The company would apply the strategy of creating their own recording label with other groups, but, at the time this book is written, JStorm consolidated as the most important Johnny's label, managing the productions of most of the company's groups.

4 The show is still on the air at the time of the analysis in 2023, but changed the title after the death of the main presenter, Shimura Ken. In September 2020, it transformed into *Minna no Dōbutsuen* and Aiba became the central *tarento* of the show.

5 Sakurai studied Economics at a prestigious private university, Keio. He graduated in 2004.

6 Lukács (2010: 214) says that since the second half of the 1990s, a rating of 15 points, representing the 15 per cent of the population, defines a hit programme and more than 20 points mean a mega-hit.

7 The use of this stadium for concerts had been restricted in different ways and it was continuously said in the media that only the top Japanese singers got permission for using it. Before Arashi, only two other groups had held concerts there: a duet called *Dreams come true* and *SMAP*, a senior group of Johnny's Jimusho.

Chapter 3

1 The show had different seasons and time slots. From October to December 1991 (Sundays 6.30 pm to 7.00 pm), and from April 1994 to March 1996 (Mondays 6.30 pm to 7.00 pm) it had the original title. Between January 1992 and March 1994 (Mondays 6.30 pm to 7.00 pm), the title changed to *Ai rabu SMAP! Dengeki kizzutai*. The titles play with the pronunciation of the kanji *ai* (love), the pronoun 'I' in English, and the Japanese pronunciation of love written in katakana (*rabu*); thus, the titles can be styled as *I love SMAP!* Or *Love love SMAP!*

2 Between 1997 and 2003, Johnny's Jimusho created a temporary unit called J-friends, consisting of three of the groups that debuted after SMAP: TOKIO, V6 and Kinki Kids. J-friends released six singles and held concerts and events

to get funds to help the victims of the earthquake and the rebuilding of the region. These groups were also chosen as leading personalities in the 24-hour TV in 1997 (Kink Kids), 1998 (TOKIO) and 2000 (V6) (Sanpo.com 2004). Thus, the involvement of Johnny's idols with charities became part of the company's regular strategies.

3   Matsumoto Jun in 2008, Sakurai Sho in 2009, and Ohno Satoshi in 2011.

4   Original in Japanese: 今自分たちがやるべきことは、きっと日本人である自分自身にきちんと誇りを持つこと。私たちが住むこの日本には、優しさと誠実さにあふれた実直な人々がたくさんいます。都会の生活なかでは見えにくくなってしまった、そんな人々に嵐のメンバーは今回の旅を通じて会ってきました。[...]日本に優しい嵐を巻き起こせるのだと、そう信じて。

5   An English version was released on METI's official website but has since been deleted. The textual citation keeps the grammar and style printed on the original source.

6   http://www.jnto.go.jp/ (video no longer available).

7   Original in Japanese: 雨降る日があるから虹が出る 苦しみぬくから強くなる 進む道も夢の地図も すべては心の中にある[...]それはふるさと。巡りあいたい人がそこにいる やさしさ広げて待っている 山も風も海の色も いちばん素直になれる場所 [...]僕のふるさと ここはふるさと。

8   In Japanese, 櫻井翔&池上彰 教科書で学べない戦争.

9   For an anaysis on the case of female idols, see Galbraith (2018); for the case of football stars, see Mandujano (2014b), Mandujano-Salazar (2023).

Chapter 4

1   It is common to hear some *tarento* – comedians and sometimes others too – being characterized according to two roles: the *boke* – funny/silly one – and the *tsukkomi* – the smart one that picks on the *boke*. These roles are taken from the Japanese comedy culture of the *manzai*.

2   This term refers to a type of personality that is normally seen as exposing more *amae* and, as long as these people are loyal and hard-working when they need to be, it does not contradict the virtues of Japaneseness. It should not be seen as the individualistic attitude that is so condemned by Japanese tradition.

3   *Otaku* in Japan, in this context, refers to people obsessed with video games, *anime, manga* and mostly antisocial attitudes.

4   In Japan, getting a degree from a prominent university is regarded as one of the main indicators of potential success and social status; Sakurai was the first idol to get a university degree – in Economics – from Keio University, something that made him suitable to become newscaster – the intellectual elite in Japanese media.

5   Nagasae was accepted and entered Meiji Gakuin University to study Sociology in 2017. When writing this, there has not been news of his graduation.

Chapter 5

1   Although tickets for the national idols' tours are highly valued and resellers try to get them, Johnny's Jimusho is much more careful when assigning them. It is known by fans' experiences that those who have many years in their fan clubs are the ones who get those.

Conclusion

1   For example, Arashi's Sakurai is the son of a bureaucrat and an academic; Hey! Say! JUMP's ex-member, Okamoto Keito is the son of Otokogumi's Okamoto Kenichi and they performed together in some Johnny's Countdown; Sexy Zone's ex-member Marius Yo is the son of a former Takarazuka actress and his father, a German national, is said to have very successful company; SixTONES's Kyomoto is the son of Kyomoto Masaki, an actor and singer, and Yamamoto Hiromi, a former female idol.

References

Alexander, J. C. (2010), 'The Celebrity-Icon', *Cultural Sociology*, 4 (3): 323–36.

ANNnews (2023), 'Moto Janīzu Jr. Ga Hō Seibi Wo Uttae. "Seikagai" Jimusho No Shazai Dōga Ni Wa [Former Johnny's Jr. Appeals for Legislation. Response to the Apology Video Regarding the 'Sexual Assault']', *YouTube*, Available online: https://www.youtube.com/watch?v=_h2w5TA4Orw (accessed 15 May 2023).

Aoki, K., A. Ootake and A. Ogasawara (2022), 'On-Screen Gender Balance in Japanese Television Programs', Tokyo: NHK Broadcasting Culture Research Institute, Available online: https://www.nhk.or.jp/bunken/research/domestic/20220501_7.html (accessed 1 May 2022).

Aoyagi, H. (2000), 'Pop Idol and the Asian Identity', in T. Craig (ed), *Japan Pop!: Inside the World of Japanese Popular Culture*, 309–26, New York: M.E. Sharpe.

Aoyagi, H. (2005), *Islands of Eight Million Smiles. Idol Performance and Symbolic Production in Contemporary Japan*, Cambridge, MA: Harvard University Asia Center.

Aoyagi, H. and M. Kovacic (2021), 'On Popular Idolatry: A Reflexive Symbological Spin', in H. Aoyagi, P. Galbraith and M. Kovacic (eds), *Idology in Transcultural Perspective*, 17–46, Cham: Springer International Publishing.

Aoyagi, H., P. W. Galbraith and M. Kovacic (2021), 'Idology in Transcultural Perspective: Anthropological Investigations of Popular Idolatry', in H. Aoyagi, P. Galbraith and M. Kovacic (eds), *Idology in Transcultural Perspective*, 1–16, Palgrave Macmillan.

Aramaki, H. (2019), '45-Nen de Nihonjin Wa Dō Kawatta Ka (1) [How Japanese Have Changed in 45 Years (1)]', *NHK Broadcasting Culture Research Institute*, Available online: https://www.nhk.or.jp/bunken/research/yoron/20190501_7.html (accessed 1 May 2019).

Arashi (2011), *Nippon No Arashi Poketto-Ban [The Arashi of Japan Pocket Edition]*, Tokyo: M.Co.

Atkins, T. (2000), 'Can Japanese Sing the Blues? "Japanese Jazz" and the Problem of Authenticity', in T. Craig (ed), *Japan Pop!: Inside the World of Japanese Popular Culture*, 27–59, New York: M.E. Sharpe.

Azhar, M. (2023), 'BBC Two - Predator: The Secret Scandal of J-Pop', *BBC Two*, Available online: https://www.bbc.co.uk/programmes/m001jw7y (accessed 10 March 2023).

Bacon, A. M. (2010), *Japanese Girls and Women*, Boston and New York: Project Gutenberg Ebook.

Barthes, R. (1977), *Image, Music, Text*, London: Fontana Press.

Barthes, R. (1999), *Mitologías, The Modern Language Journal*, México: Siglo XXI.

BBC News (2011), 'Japan Pop Band SMAP in Rare Beijing Concert', *BBC News*, Available online: https://www.bbc.com/news/world-asia-pacific-14945963 (accessed 21 February 2023).

BBC News Japan (2023), 'BBC, Ko Jani Kitagawa-Shi No Kagai Ni Tsuite Shuzai Kotoba Wo Tsumaraseru Moto Junia [Interview on the Perpetration of the Late Johnny Kitagawa, a Former Junior Who Is at a Loss for Words]', *BBC News Japan*, Available online: https://www.bbc.com/japanese/video-64859230 (accessed 2 April 2023).

Befu, H. (2001), *Hegemony of Homogeneity: An Anthropological Analysis of Nihonjinron*, Melbourne: Trans Pacific Press.

Belk, R. W., M. Wallendorf and J. F. Sherry (1989), 'The Sacred and the Profane in Consumer Behavior: Theodicy on the Odyssey', *Journal of consumer Research*, 16 (1): 1–38.

Bengoshi Dot Com News (2023), 'Janīzu-Sei Kagai Mondai, Shūkanbunshun Henshū-Chō Ga Shiteki Suru. Media to Jimusho No Rieki Kyōdōtai [Johnny's Persecution Problem, Weekly Bunshun Editor-in-Chief Points out That There Are Common Interests between Media and Talent Companies]', *Yahoo! Japan News*, Available online: https://news.yahoo.co.jp/articles/d4d5bf2d8f7aa5abdaedc8aed9edf06073032e9b (accessed 14 April 2023).

Benoza, K. and K. Takahara (2023), 'Major Japanese Talent Agency Apologizes over Sexual Assault Claims', *The Japan Times*, Available online: https://www.japantimes.co.jp/culture/2023/05/14/entertainment-news/johhny-associates-president-apology/ (accessed 13 May 2023).

Billboard Japan (2023), 'King & Prince Life Goes On/We Are Young 2-Saku Renzoku Mirion Toppa [King & Prince Life Goes on/We Are Young 2 Consecutive Million Breakthroughs]', *Billboard Japan*, Available online: https://www.billboard-japan.com/d_news/detail/122272/ (accessed 31 March 2023).

Billig, M. (1995), *Banal Nationalism*, London: SAGE Publications.

Boorstin, D. J. (1992), *The Image: A Guide to Pseudo-Events in America*, New York: Vintage Books.

Box Office Mojo (2009), 'Japanese Box Office Weekends for 2008', *Box Office Mojo*, Available online: https://www.boxofficemojo.com/weekend/by-year/2008/?area=JP&sort=gross&ref_=bo_wey__resort#table (accessed 11 February 2023).

Brasor, P. (2019), 'Idols and Agencies in Japan Navigate a Brand New Landscape', *The Japan Times*, Available online: https://www.japantimes.co.jp/news/2019/03/23/national/media-national/idols-agencies-japan-navigate-brand-new-landscape/ (accessed 1 April 2023).

Bunshun Online (2022), 'Takkī Seiken No Shissaku. Janīzu Kara Kokuminteki Aidoru Ga Zetsumetsu Shita Hontō No Riyū. Kinpuri Hirano & Nagase Ga Kagi o Nigitte Iru [Mistake of the Tackey Administration. The Real Reason Why National Idols Disappeared from Johnny's. King & Prince's Hirano & Nagase Hold the Key]', *Bunshun Online*, Available online: https://bunshun.jp/articles/-/50988 (accessed 24 February 2023).

Bunshun Online (2023), 'BBC Janī Kitagawa-Shi-Sei Kagai Kokuhatsu Bangumi Zen Sekai Hōsō He Hakkaku No Genten Shūkanbunshun 1999-Nen Junia He No Sekuhara Kokuhatsu Kiji Wo Sai Kōkai [BBC Johnny Kitagawa's Sexual Harassment Accusation Program to Broadcast Worldwide Shuukan Bunshun 1999 Re-Published Article Accusing Juniors of Sexual Harassment]', *Yahoo! Japan News*, Available online: https://news.yahoo.co.jp/articles/d236028c9430e6a8a579b714f61ed6fa3e41ee58 (accessed 17 March 2023).

CD Journal (2023), 'King & Prince, Besuto Arubamu Ga Hatsu Shū Mirion Tassei Dansei Ātisuto Shijō 9 Kumime & Konnendo-Hatsu [King & Prince's Best-of Album Hits Million Mark in the First Week; Ninth Male Artist Group in History & First This Year]', *Yahoo! Japan News*, Available online: https://news.yahoo.co.jp/articles/6bbe724f60973cf614876a42be791cc3a2509604 (accessed 24 April 2023).

CGTN (2019), 'Johnny Kitagawa, the Man Who Shaped Japanese Entertainment, Dies at 87', *CGTN*, Available online: https://news.cgtn.com/news/2019-07-10/Johnny-Kitagawa-the-man-who-shaped-Japanese-entertainment-dies-at-87-IdkiXZfSE0/index.html (accessed 1 April 2023).

Chon, C. (2023), 'Tonari No Heya Ni Ryōshin Ga Iru No Ni … Ko Janī Kitagawashi, Miseinensha e No Seiteki Gyakutai Bakurosareru [Eventhough My Parents Were in the next Room … The Late Johnny Kitagawa Exposed for Sexual Abuse of Minors]', *Chosun Online*, Available online: https://news.yahoo.co.jp/articles/cfd9a8b77907b1bf0cb3cc96ec90cb163acbef63 (accessed 10 March 2023).

Chunichi Post (2022), 'Nino Ga 2-Ji No Papa Ni Dai 2-Ko to Naru Jijo Tanjō Wo Hōkoku Atarashī Kazoku Ga Fuete Nigiyaka Ni Naru Koto Ni Yorokobi Wo Kanjite Orimasu [Nino Announces the Birth of Her Second Daughter to the Father of Two Children "I Feel Happy That the New Family Will Increase and Become Lively"]', *Chunichi Post*, Available online: https://www.chunichi.co.jp/article/585449 (accessed 27 February 2023).

CNTV (2011), 'Japanese Pop Group SMAP Holds 1st Overseas Concert in Beijin', *China.org.cn*, Available online: http://www.china.org.cn/video/2011-09/17/content_23438112.htm (accessed 21 February 2023).

Cool Japan Advisory Council (2011), 'Creating a New Japan. Tying Together "culture and Industry" and "Japan and the World"', *Ministry of Economy, Trade and Industry*, Available online: http://www.meti.go.jp/english/press/2011/pdf/0512_02b.pdf (accessed 12 May 2011).

Creative Industries Division Ministry of Economy Trade and Industry (2012), 'Cool Japan Strategy', *Ministry of Economy, Trade and Industry*, Available online: https://www.meti.go.jp/english/policy/mono_info_service/creative_industries/pdf/120116_01a.pdf (accessed 16 January 2012).

Cyzo Woman (2022), 'Arashi Aibamasaki, Papa Ni Naru Shūkanshi Hōdō Mo … ninshin Sukūpu Yamete Nani Ka Attara Dō Suru No? Kugen Zokushutsu [Arashi's Aiba Masaki Becoming a Dad According to Weekly Magazine Report … "Stop Pregnancy Scope, What If Something Happens?"]', *Cyzo Woman*, Available online: https://www.cyzowoman.com/2022/08/post_397709_1.html (accessed 27 February 2023).

Cyzo Woman Henshubu (2023), 'Moto Janīzu Junia Ga Kataru, Janī Kitagawashi No Sei Gyakutai Kokuhatsu Ga Sukunasugiru Wake [Former Johnny's Junior Talks about Johnny Kitagawa's Sexual Abuse Accusations]', *Cyzo Woman*, Available online: https://www.cyzowoman.com/2023/03/post_425384_1.html (accessed 10 March 2023).

Darling-Wolf, F. (2004), 'SMAP, Sex, and Masculinity: Constructing the Perfect Female Fantasy in Japanese Popular Music', *Popular Music and Society*, 27 (3): 357–70.

Dasgupta, R. (2010), 'Globalisation and the Bodily Performance of "Cool" and "Un-Cool" Masculinities in Corporate Japan', *Intersections: Gender and Sexuality in Asia and the Pacific* (23), http://intersections.anu.edu.au/issue23/dasgupta.htm.

Debord, G. (1977), *The Society of the Spectacle*, Detroit: Black & Red.

Delanty, G. (1999), 'Self, Other and World: Discourses of Nationalism and Cosmopolitanism', *Cultural Values*, 3 (3): 365–75.

Desser, D. (1995), 'From the Opium War to the Pacific War: Japanese Propaganda Films of the World War II', *Film History*, 7 (1): 45–6.

Digital Business Lab (2022), 'Social Media Penetration in Japan [Research]', *Digital Business Lab*, Available online: https://digital-business-lab.com/2022/10/%E2%91%A1-social-media-penetration-in-japan-research/ (accessed 28 February 2023).

Doi, T. (1981), *The Anatomy of Dependence*, Tokyo: Kodansha International.

Doi, T. (1988), *The Anatomy of Self. The Individual versus Society*, Tokyo: Kodansha International.

Durkheim, E. (2012), *The Elementary Forms of the Religious Life*, London: The Project Gutenberg Ebook.

Edensor, T. (2001), 'Performing Tourism, Staging Tourism', *Tourist Studies*, 1 (1): 59–81.

Entame, K. (2023), 'Kinpuri Hirano Shō Ga Imishinna Kashi Machigai de Ketsui Hyōmei Ka? "Shindereragāru" Ni Kometa Messēji [Is King & Prince's Hirano Sho Expressing His Determination with a Meaningful Lyric Mistake? Message in "Cinderella Girl"]', *Shūkan Josei PRIME*, Available online: https://news.yahoo.co.jp/articles/11f5ad0c40d b2cb314553a4ca57350d5cc9f51b1?page=1 (accessed 4 April 2023).

Fernández, O. and R. Cachán-Cruz (2017), 'Religion in Motion: Continuities and Symbolic Affinities in Religion and Sport', *Journal of Religion and Health*, 56 (6): 1903–15.

Fiske, J. (2005), *Reading the Popular*, New York: Taylor & Francis e-Library.

Flash (2023), 'Kinpuri 5-Ri Rasuto Arubamu Genteiban Wa 4-Bai de Tenbai … Fankurabu Dōga No Kanashiki Ichimon Ni Rakutansuru Koe Mo [King & Prince's Last Album as Five Members Limited Edition Resale at 4 Times Its Original Price … There Are Also Voices of Discouragement for the Sorrow Expressed in the Fan Club Video]', *Yahoo! Japan News*, Available online: https://news.yahoo.co.jp/article s/6088f1fb3f55594a1ef42ba25f8184310cf0cca2 (accessed 19 April 2023).

Forbridge (2016), 'Kako Ni Mo Okite Ita Sumappu No Kiki Inagaki Gorō No Taiho Wo Furikaeru! [Looking Back to the Crisis of SMAP When Inagaki Goro Was Arrested!]', *Excite News*, Available online: https://www.excite.co.jp/news/article/ E1450359530349/ (accessed 23 February 2023).

Foucault, M. (1980), *Power/Knowledge. Selected Interviews and Other Writings 1972–1977*, New York: Pantheon Books.

Frühstück, S. (2022), *Gender and Sexuality in Modern Japan*, Santa Barbara: University of California.

Fuji Television (n.d.), 'Renzoku Dokyumentarī RIDE ON TIME Archives [Archives of the Serial Documentary RIDE ON TIME]', *Fuji tele view*, Available online: https://www.fujitv-view.jp/programs/ride-on-time/ (accessed 25 February 2023).

Fuji TV (n.d.), 'Johnny's Countdown', *Fuji TV*, Available online: https://www.fujitv. co.jp/j-countdown/ (accessed 31 March 2023).

Fukuda, M. (2021), 'Arashi Ninomiya Kazunari, Zettai Papa Shiteruyo Akachan Ni Seikatsu Awaseteru to Odoroki No Koe! Igaina Shiseikatsu Wo Akashite Wadai Ni [Arashi's Kazunari Ninomiya, Surprised Declaration Saying I'm Definitely a Dad and I'm Adjusting My Life to the Baby! The Unexpected Revelations of His Private Life Became a Hot Topic]', *Cyzo Woman*, Available online: https://www. cyzowoman.com/2021/07/post_351443_1.html (accessed 27 February 2023).

Fukui, S. (2019), 'Arashi Katsudō Kyūshi. Kaiken Zenbun. Rīdā No Seide Wanai (Ninomiya) Hajimete Kiita Toki Wa Hikkurikaetta (Aiba) [Arashi Suspends Activities. Full Interview. It's Not the Leader's Fault (Ninomiya) I Was Overwhelmed When I First Heard It (Aiba)]', *Aeradot*, Available online: https:// dot.asahi.com/dot/2019012700031.html?page=1 (accessed 25 February 2023).

Fukushima, G. S. (1995), 'JPRI Occasional Paper No. 2', *The Great Hanshin Earthquake*, Available online: https://jpri.org/wp-content/uploads/2021/11/Occasional-Paper-02.pdf (accessed 21 February 2023).

Galbraith, P. W. (2012), 'Idols: The Image of Desire in Japanese Consumer Capitalism', in P. W. Galbraith and J. G. Karlin (eds), *Idols and Celebrity in Japanese Media Culture*, 185–208, London: Palgrave Macmillan UK.

Galbraith, P. W. (2018), 'National Idols', in F. Darling-Wolf (ed), *Routledge Handbook of Japanese Media*, 136–53, London: Routledge.

Galbraith, P. W. (2021), 'Idol Economics: Television, Affective and Virtual Models in Japan', in H. Aoyagi, P. Galbraith and M. Kovacic (eds), *Idology in Transcultural Perspective*, 65–89, Cham: Palgrave Macmillan.

Galbraith, P. W. and J. G. Karlin (2012), 'Introduction: The Mirror of Idols and Celebrity', in P. W. Galbraith and J. G. Karlin (eds), *Idols and Celebrity in Japanese Media Culture*, 1–32, London: Palgrave Macmillan UK.

Geinō Dasshu (2023), 'Kiken Shingō. Kinpuri Nagase Kotoba Ga Denai Karō de Genkai Ka?! Jurī Wa Kinpuri o Tōhōshinki No Yō Ni Shitai?! Nado Dokuji Jōhō Mo Majie Tettei Kaisetsu! [Dangerous Signal. King & Prince Nagase "I Have No Words" Is He Overworked?! Julie Wants to Make King & Prince like Tohoshinki?! Thorough Explanation with Unique Information]', *YouTube*, Available online: https://www.youtube.com/watch?v=hRxrr56dA_4 (accessed 3 April 2023).

Gellner, E. (1983), *Nations and Nationalism*, New York: Cornell University Press.

Goo Ranking (2016), 'Fan Wa Shinderera!? Sexy Zone's Nakajima Kento No Ōjisama Sugiru Densetsu Rankingu [Fans Are Cinderella!? The Ranking of Legends about Sexy Zone's Nakajima Kento's Prince Behaviour]', *Goo Ranking*, Available online: https://ranking.goo.ne.jp/column/3602/ (accessed 4 March 2023).

Gordon, A. (2003), *A Modern History of Japan: From Tokugawa Times to the Present*, Oxford: Oxford University Press.

Gossmann, H. (2000), 'New Role Models for Men and Women? Gender in Japanese TV Dramas', in T. Craig (ed), *Japan Pop!: Inside the World of Japanese Popular Culture*, 207–21, New York: M.E. Sharpe.

Grossberg, L. (2001), 'Is There a Fan in the House?: The Affective Sensibility of Fandom', in L. A. Lewis (ed), *The Adoring Audience: Fan Culture and Popular Media*, 50–65, New York: Taylor & Francis e-Library.

Han, B.-C. (2017), *Psychopolitics: Neoliberalism and New Technologies of Power*, Verso.

Hayashi, R. (2019), 'Arashi to Go Full Throttle on Social Media a Year before Hiatus', *The Asahi Shimbun*, Available online: https://www.asahi.com/ajw/articles/13057422 (accessed 18 February 2023).

Hidaka, T. (2010), *Salaryman Masculinity: The Continuity of and Change in the Hegemonic Masculinity in Japan*, Leiden: Brill.

Holmes, S. and S. Redmond (2010), 'A Journal in Celebrity Studies', *Celebrity Studies*, 1 (1): 1–10.

Hotaka, T. and E. Asoda (2021), 'Koronaka Wa Terebi to Dōga No Riyōsha Ni Donna Eikyō Wo Ataeta Ka Korona Jidai No Terebi No Kachi Chōsa No Kekka Kara [What Kind of Impact Did the Corona Disaster Have on TV and Video Users? Results from the Survey on Value of TV in the Corona Era]', *NHK Broadcasting Culture Research Institute*, Available online: https://www.nhk.or.jp/bunken/research/domestic/pdf/20211001_8.pdf (accessed 1 October 2021).

IFPI (2022), 'Global Music Report', Available online: https://www.ifpi.org/wp-content/uploads/2022/04/IFPI_Global_Music_Report_2022-State_of_the_Industry.pdf (accessed April 2022).

Iida, Y. (2002), *Rethinking Identity in Modern Japan: Nationalism as Aesthetics*, London: Routledge.

Ivy, M. (1993), 'Formations of Mass Culture', in A. Gordon (ed), *Postwar Japan as History*, 239–58, Los Angeles: University of California Press.

Iwabuchi, K. (2002), *Recentering Globalization: Popular Culture and Japanese Transnationalism*, Durham and London: Duke University Press.

J Storm Inc (n.d.), 'JStorm', *JStorm*, Available online: https://www.j-storm.co.jp/ (accessed 12 February 2023).

Jackson, E. (1989), 'Kabuki Narratives of Male Homoerotic Desire in Saikaku and Mishima', *Theatre Journal*, 41 (4): 459–77.

Jackson, R. (2016), 'Homosocial Mentorship and the Serviceable Female Corpse: Manhood Rituals in "The Tale of Genji"', *Harvard Journal of Asiatic Studies*, 76 (1–2): 1–41.

Jackson, R. (2019), 'Desiring Spectacular Discipline: Aspiration, Fraternal Anxiety, and the Allure of Restraint in Nō's Dōjōji', *Asian Theatre Journal*, 26 (1): 47–78.

Japan Airlines (2010), 'Tokubetsu Tosō-Ki Jaru Arashi Jetto Ga Shūkō! [Special Painting Plane JAL Arashi JET Goes into Service!]', *Japan Airlines Press Releases*, Available online: https://press.jal.co.jp/ja/release/201009/001075.html (accessed 17 February 2023).

Japan Airlines (2011), 'Tokubetsu tosōki Kaibutsukun JET 11gatsu tsuitachi shūkō [Special Painting Plane Kaibutsukun JET Goes into Service on November first]', *Japan Airlines Press Releases*, Available online: http://press.jal.co.jp/ja/bw_uploads/JGN11098.pdf (accessed 17 February 2023).

Japan Airlines (2012), 'Tokubetsu dekaruki JAL Arashi JET dai 3 dan honjitsu shūkō [Special Decorated Plane JAL Arashi JET Number 3 Goes into Service Today]', *Japan Airlines Press Releases,* Available online: http://press.jal.co.jp/ja/bw_uploads/MjAxMjEwMjNfSkdOMTIxMjhfk8GVyoNmg0qBW4OLi0CBdUpBTJeS SkVUgXaR5jOSZSCWe5P6j0G NcS5wZGY.pdf (accessed 17 February 2023).

Japan Airlines (2015), 'JAL FLY to 2020 tokubetsu tosōki ga kokunai ni shūkō [Special Painting Plane JAL FLY to 2020 Goes into Service nationally]', *Japan Airlines Press Releases*, Available online: http://press.jal.co.jp/ja/bw_uploads/ MjAxNTA2MjZfSkdOMTUwNjJfSkFMIEZseSB0byAyMDIwIJPBlcqTaJG Vi0BfLnBkZ g.pdf (accessed 17 February 2023).

J-Cast News (2009), 'Deisui Taiho No Sumappu Kusanagi Imi Fumeina Sakebi No Wake [SMAP's Kusanagi Arrested for Being Drunk and Scream]', *J-Cast News*, Available online: https://www.j-cast.com/2009/04/23040072.html?p=all (accessed 23 February 2023).

Jindra, M. (1994), 'Star Trek Fandom as a Religious Phenomenon', *Sociology of Religion*, 55 (1): 27.

Johnny & Associates (2023a), 'Johnny's Net', *Johnny's Net*, Available online: https:// www.johnnys-net.jp/ (accessed 10 February 2023).

Johnny & Associates (2023b), 'Ko Janī Kitagawa Ni Yoru Sei Kagai Mondai Ni Tsuite Tōsha No Kenkai to Taiō [Our View and Response to the Sexual Assault Issue by the Late Johnny Kitagawa]', *Johnny & Associates*, Available online: https://www. johnny-associates.co.jp/news/info-700/ (accessed 13 May 2023).

Joho Station Tokuneta (2019), 'Janī Kitagawa Wa Sei Hanzai-Sha? Gō Hiromi Arashi SMAP Saiban No Shinjitsu Wa? [Is Johnny Kitagawa a Sex Offender? Go Hiromi, Arashi, SMAP's Trial Truth?', *Joho Station Tokuneta*, Available online: https:// tokuneta.info/archives/7333 (accessed 10 March 2023).

Josei Jishin Henshubu (2023), 'Takizawa Hideakishi Shingaisha Setsuritsu No Tokushuna Ōbo Yōkō Ni Ryūkō No Ōdishon Bangumi Kitai Suru Koe [The Voice of Expectation for Takizawa Hideaki's New Company Establishment's Special Subscription as a Popular Audition Program]', *Josei Jishin*, Available online: https:// jisin.jp/entertainment/entertainment-news/2188720/ (accessed 31 March 2023).

Kaneko, K. and K. Takahara (2023), 'Johnny's Replaces President as It Admits to Abuse by Late Founder', *The Japan Times*, Available online: https://www. japantimes.co.jp/news/2023/09/07/japan/society/johnnys-new-president/ (accessed 6 September 2023).

Kanko Keizai Shinbun (2010), 'Hōnichi Kankō PR Ni Arashi Kiyō [Using Arashi for Sightseeing PR Visiting Japan]', *Kankokeizai.com*, Available online: https:// www.kankokeizai.com/backnumber/10/04_17/kanko_gyosei.html (accessed 17 February 2023).

Kankōchō (2010a), 'Arashi × Kankō-Chō Kankō Rikkoku Nabigētā to Shite Arashi Wo Kiyō! [Arashi x Japan Tourism Agency. Arashi Appointed as National Tourism Navigator!]', *Kankōchō*, Available online: http://www.mlit.go.jp/kankocho/en/ news01_000038.html (accessed 17 February 2023).

Kankōchō (2010b), 'Kankō Puromōshon in Hanedakūkō No Jisshi Dantai Ga Kettei! [It Was Decided to Implement Organizations for Tourism Promotion in

Haneda Airport]', *Kankōchō*, Available online: http://www.mlit.go.jp/kankocho/news05_000059.html (accessed 17 February 2023).

Kankōchō (2010c), 'Kankō Rikkoku Nabigētā Arashi No Minasan Ni Yoru Tosho (Nippon No Arashi) No Zenkoku No Ko-Chū Kōtō Gakkōnado He No Kizō e No Kyōryoku Ni Tsuite [Cooperation in Donating Books (The Arashi of Japan) to Elementary, Junior High and High Schools Nationwide]', *Kankōchō*, Available online: http://www.mlit.go.jp/kankocho/news08_000048.html (accessed 17 February 2023).

Karlin, J. G. (2012), 'Through a Looking Glass Darkly: Television Advertising, Idols, and the Making of Fan Audiences', in P. W. Galbraith and J. G. Karlin (eds), *Idols and Celebrity in Japanese Media Culture*, 72–93, London: Palgrave Macmillan UK.

Kei, K., T. Koichi and H. Miwako (2010), 'The Survey of Japanese Value Orientations: Analysis of Trends over Thirty-Five Years', *NHK Broadcasting Studies*, 8: 1–62. Available online: https://www.nhk.or.jp/bunken/english/reports/pdf/10_no8_04.pdf.

Keisai Sangyōshō (2021), 'Cool Japan Kikō Ni Tsuite [About the Mechanism of Cool Japan]', *Ministry of Economy, Trade and Industry*, Available online: https://www.meti.go.jp/policy/mono_info_service/mono/creative/2110CoolJapanFundr1.pdf (accessed October 2021).

Kelman, H. C. (2011), 'Nationalism and National Identity: A Social-Psychological Analysis', in M. Abou-Taam, J. Esser and N. Foroutan (eds), *Zwischen Konfrontation Und Dialog*, 23–50, Wiesbaden: VS Verlag für Sozialwissenschaften.

Kikuchi, D. (2016), 'Love'em or Hate'em, the End of SMAP Marks the End of an Era', *The Japan Times*, Available online: https://www.japantimes.co.jp/culture/2016/12/25/music/love-em-hate-em-end-smap-marks-end-era/ (accessed 22 February 2023).

Kimura, M. (2012), 'Arashi-Ryu Global Katsudō, Sono Kangaekata', *Nikkei Entertainment*, September: 70–80.

King & Prince (2022), 'King & Prince CD Debyū 4-Shūnen Kōshiki SNS Kaisetsu 1 Shūnenkinen [King & Prince 4th Anniversary of CD Debut and 1st Anniversary of Official SNS Opening]', *YouTube*, Available online: https://www.youtube.com/watch?v=Y-LXA9o3spY (accessed 28 April 2023).

Koh, L. (2019), 'Japanese Boyband Mogul Johnny Kitagawa Passes Away at 87', *The Independent Singapore*, Available online: https://theindependent.sg/japanese-boyband-mogul-johnny-kitagawa-passes-away-at-87/ (accessed 1 April 2023).

KP Information (2023), '2023-Nen 2 Tsuki Saishinban Janīzufankurabu Kaiinsū Matome [February 2023 Latest Version. Summary of Johnny's Fan Club Members]', *King & Prince Saishin Joho*, Available online: https://kpinformation.jp/?p=4860 (accessed 25 February 2023).

Kurihara, Y. (2016), 'Naze Sumappu Wa Kokuminteki Aidoru to Yoba Reta No Ka [Why Was SMAP Called a National Idol?]', *Toyo Keizai Online*, Available online: https://toyokeizai.net/articles/-/151844 (accessed 21 February 2023).

Kurokawa, C. (2010), 'Social Frameworks for Civil Society in Japan: In Search for a Japanese Model', in H. Vinken, Y. Nishimura, B. L. White and M. Deguchi (eds), *Civil Engagement in Contemporary Japan: Established and Emerging Repertoires*, 41–64, New York: Springer.

Kyodo (2019a), 'Arashi to Hold Two Concerts at the New National Stadium in Lead-up to Tokyo Games', *The Japan Times*, Available online: https://www.japantimes. co.jp/culture/2019/11/03/entertainment-news/arashi-hold-2-concerts-new-national-stadium-lead-tokyo-games/ (accessed 28 April 2023).

Kyodo (2019b), 'Idol Group Arashi Sing at Festival Held to Mark Emperor's Enthronement', *The Japan Times*, Available online: https://www.japantimes.co.jp/ news/2019/11/09/national/idol-group-arashi-sing-festival-held-mark-emperors-enthronement/ (accessed 21 February 2023).

Kyodo (2020), 'Tomoya Nagase to Leave Tokio in March, Bringing Japan Boy Band's Founding Five to Three', *The Japan Times*, Available online: https://www. japantimes.co.jp/culture/2020/07/23/entertainment-news/tomoya-nagase-tokio/ (accessed 1 April 2023).

Kyodo (2023), 'Japan OKs Bill to Reform Sexual Offense Charge and Raise Age of Consent', *The Japan Times*, Available online: https://www.japantimes.co.jp/ news/2023/03/14/national/sexual-offenses-bill/ (accessed 9 May 2023).

Kyodo News (2020a), 'Japan Pop Group Arashi Performs Solo in Empty Olympic Stadium', *Kyodo News*, Available online: https://english.kyodonews.net/ news/2020/11/ce0142acd376-japan-pop-group-arashi-performs-solo-in-empty-olympic-stadium.html (accessed 28 April 2023).

Kyodo News (2020b), '38% of LGBT People in Japan Sexually Harassed or Assaulted: Survey', *Kyodo News*, Available online: https://english.kyodonews.net/ news/2020/12/2cfe9ff21ca8-38-of-lgbt-people-sexually-harassed-or-assaulted-survey.html (accessed 15 October 2022).

Lebra, T. S. (2004), *The Japanese Self in Cultural Logic*, Hawaii: University of Hawaii Press.

Löbert, A. (2012), 'Fandom as a Religious Form: On the Reception of Pop Music by Cliff Richard Fans in Liverpool', *Popular Music*, 31 (1): 125–41.

Lu, L. Y. (2020), 'Arashi Members Explain Heartbreaking Decision for Hiatus in Netflix Documentary', *Yahoo! Lifestyle Singapore*, Available online: https://sg.style. yahoo.com/arashi-members-explain-heartbreaking-decision-for-hiatus-in-netflix-documentary-115748894.html (accessed 24 February 2023).

Lukács, G. (2010), *Scripted Affects, Branded Selves: Television, Subjectivity, and Capitalism in 1990s Japan*, Durham: Duke University Press.

MacDuff, W. (1996), 'Beautiful Boys in Nō Drama: The Idealization of Homoerotic Desire', *Asian Theatre Journal*, 13 (2): 248–58.

Mainichi Japan (2022), 'Editorial: Japan's Legal Penalties for Sex Crimes Need Further Review', *The Mainichi*, Available online: https://mainichi.jp/english/articles/20221029/p2a/00m/0op/010000c (accessed 9 May 2023).

Mandujano, Y. (2014a), 'Flagging the National Identity, Reinforcing Japaneseness', *Electronic Journal of Contemporary Japanese Studies*, 14 (1). https://www.japanesestudies.org.uk/ejcjs/vol14/iss1/mandujano.html

Mandujano, Y. (2014b), 'Japanese Media Ideologies behind the National Football Teams', *Electronic Journal of Contemporary Japanese Studies*, 14 (1): Discussion Paper 2. https://www.japanesestudies.org.uk/ejcjs/vol14/iss1/mandujano1.html

Mandujano-Salazar, Y. Y. (2009), 'El Mercado de IDOL Varones En Japón, 1999–2008: Caracterización de La Oferta a Través Del Estudio de Un Caso Representativo', in *Master*, Mexico: El Colegio de México.

Mandujano-Salazar, Y. Y. (2014), 'Media Idols and National "Representation": Strengthening the National Identity in Contemporary Japan', Doctoral dissertation, Universidad Autónoma de Ciudad Juárez.

Mandujano-Salazar, Y. Y. (2016), 'The War That Cannot Be Learned from Textbooks or the National Identity Discourse That Can Be Perceived in Media?', *Electronic Journal of Contemporary Japanese Studies*, 16 (1). https://www.japanesestudies.org.uk/ejcjs/vol16/iss1/mandujano-salazar.html

Mandujano-Salazar, Y. Y. (2017), 'It Is Not That I Can't, It Is That I Won't: The Struggle of Japanese Women to Redefine Female Singlehood through Television Dramas', *Asian Studies Review*, 41 (4): 526–43.

Mandujano-Salazar, Y. Y. (2018), 'Media Idols and the Regime of Truth about National Identity in Post-3.11 Japan', in F. Darling-Wolf (ed), *Routledge Handbook of Japanese Media*, 154–66, New York: Routledge.

Mandujano-Salazar, Y. Y. (2020), 'Pop Idols, Mediatized Places, and Identity-Oriented Performances of Fans as Domestic Tourists in Japan', in M. Månsson, A. Buchmann, C. Cassinger and L. Eskilsson (eds), *The Routledge Companion to Media and Tourism*, 92–101, London: Routledge.

Mandujano-Salazar, Y. Y. (2024), 'The Gender-Related Discursive Function of Japanese Football since Its Professionalization', in H. Macnaughtan and V. Postlethwaite (eds), *Handbook of Sport and Japan*, Tokyo: MHM Limited.

Marshall, P. D. (1997), *Celebrity and Power: Fame in Contemporary Culture*, Amsterdam: Amsterdam University Press.

Marx, D. W. (2012), 'The Jimusho System: Understanding the Production Logic of the Japanese Entertainment Industry', in P. W. Galbraith and J. G. Karlin (eds), *Idols and Celebrity in Japanese Media Culture*, 35–55, London: Palgrave Macmillan UK.

Matsutani, K. (2022), 'Janīzu Wa Taisho Rasshu Daga … Kinpuri 3 Ri Dattai Ga Ketteiteki Ni Chigau Wake [Johnny's Is in a Retirement Rush, but … the Reason Why King & Prince's Withdrawal Is Definitely Different]', *Bunshun Online*, Available online: https://bunshun.jp/articles/-/58863 (accessed 24 February 2023).

Matsutani, K. (2023), 'Janīzu Jimusho No Saidai No Kyōhan-Sha Terebikyoku Wa, Jiko Kenshō o Sakete Wa Naranai [Johnny's Office's Biggest Accomplices, TV Stations Must Not Avoid Self-Verification]', *Yahoo! Japan News*, Available online: https://news.yahoo.co.jp/expert/articles/ cd76d95b3d7835b64bf8f6453b1977a696bbd8a0 (accessed 30 August 2023).

McLellan, M. (2008), 'Male Homosexuality and Popular Culture in Modern Japan', *Intersections: Gender, history and culture in the Asian context* (3), http:// intersections.anu.edu.au/issue3/mclelland2.html.

McLelland, M. and K. Suganuma (2009), 'Sexual Minorities and Human Rights in Japan: An Historical Perspective', *The International Journal of Human Rights*, 13 (2–3): 329–43.

Ministry of Economy Trade and Industry (2013), 'Act on Establishment of the Japan Brand Fund Was Passed by the Diet and Promulgated', *METI Ministry of Economy, Trade and Industry*, Available online: http://www.meti.go.jp/english/ press/2013/0708_01.html (accessed 12 July 2013).

Miyao, D. (2002), 'Before Anime: Animation and the Pure Film Movement in Pre-War Japan', *Japan Forum*, 14 (2): 191–209.

Model Press (2013), 'Arashi Kara Saigo No Messēji Himitsu No Arashi-Chan 5-Nen No Rekishi Ni Maku [Last Message from Arashi's 5-Year History of Himitsu No Arashi-Chan]', *Model Press*, Available online: https://mdpr.jp/news/detail/1231131 (accessed 10 March 2023).

Model Press (2019), 'King & Prince, Janīzu-Hatsu No Kaikyo Ni Yorokobi GQ Men OF THE YEAR 2019 [King & Prince, Delighted to Be Johnny's First Group Featured as GQ MEN OF THE YEAR 2019]', *Model Press*, Available online: https://mdpr.jp/news/detail/1898355 (accessed 24 February 2023).

Mori Channel (2023), 'Saikin Wadai No Janī Kitagawa Ni Tsuite Katara Sete Mita [Talking about Johnny Kitagawa, Who Has Been a Hot Topic Recently]', *YouTube*, Available online: https://www.youtube.com/watch?v=WG8NVYGku8o&list=-PLskrcg1Z9o4z0Qe8Ev_V-o78lCFv9vhYs&index=10 (accessed 9 May 2023).

Morris-Suzuki, T. (2006), 'Defining the Boundaries of the Cold War Nation: 1950s Japan and the Other Within', *Japanese Studies*, 26 (3): 303–16.

Moscovici, S. (1986), *Psicología Social II. Pensamiento y Vida Social: Psicología Social y Problemas Sociales*, Barcelona: Paidós.

Nagaike, K. (2012), 'Johnny's Idols as Icons: Female Desires to Fantasize and Consume Male Idol Images', in P. W. Galbraith and J. G. Karlin (eds), *Idols and Celebrity in Japanese Media Culture*, 97–112, London: Palgrave Macmillan UK.

Nakamura, R. (2022), '1999-Nen Irai, Zetsubō Shi Kitte Imasu. BBC Mo Chūmoku Suru Janī Kitagawa No Seiteki Gyakutai Mondai, Nihon No Media Ga Mushisuru Wake [I've Been in Despair since 1999. Johnny Kitagawa's Sexual Abuse Issue, Which Is Also Attracting Attention from the BBC, Is Why the Japanese Media Ignores It]', *Bunshun Online*, Available online: https://bunshun.jp/articles/-/59446 (accessed 10 March 2023).

Nakane, C. (1973), *Japanese Society*, Middlesex: Penguin Books.

Nakata Atsuhiko (2023), 'Janīzu to Jidō Gyakutai (Johnny's Child Abuse) Shodai Janīzu Kara Okamoto Kauan-Shi Made Jidō Gyakutai to Kokuhatsu No Rekishi Wo Kanzen Kaisetsu [Johnny's Child Abuse. A Complete Explanation of the History of Child Abuse and Accusations from the First Johnny's to Okamoto Kowan]', *YouTube*, Available online: https://www.youtube.com/watch?v=o3B3PZZv5ig (accessed 9 May 2023).

Netflix (2019), 'Netflix Orijinaru Dokyumentarī Shirīzu ARASHI's Diary -Voyage- [Netflix Original Documentary Series ARASHI's Diary -Voyage-]', *Netflix*, Available online: https://about.netflix.com/ja/news/arashi (accessed 24 February 2023).

Netorabo (2023), 'NHK "kurōzuappu Gendai" Janī-Shi No Seikagai Mondai o Hōsō Higaishatachi No Aratana Shōgen Wo Dokuji Shuzai [NHK "Close-up Gendai" Broadcasting Johnny's Sexual Abuse Issue with Independent Coverage of Victims' New Testimonies]', *Yahoo! Japan News*, Available online: https://news.yahoo.co.jp/articles/535ba7a1efac7bbe9e554e1d1f11de3ae520c8ad (accessed 15 May 2023).

Newage Repo (n.d.), 'Janīzu Fan Kurabu Kaiinsū Rankingu 2023-Nenban [Johnny's Fan Club Membership Ranking 2023]', *Shinjidai Repo*, Available online: https://report-newage.com/18785 (accessed 25 February 2023).

Ng, K. (2023), 'Japan to Ban Upskirting in Sweeping Sex Crime Reforms', *BBC News*, Available online: https://www.bbc.com/news/world-asia-pacific-65453384 (accessed 9 May 2023).

NHK (n.d.a), 'The Shonen Club', *NHK*, Available online: https://www.nhk.jp/p/shonen/ts/8XR6MQY3W7/ (accessed 31 March 2023a).

NHK (n.d.b), 'The Shonen Club Premium', *NHK*, Available online: https://www.nhk.jp/p/shonen-p/ts/JV32KPY9VP/ (accessed 31 March 2023b).

NHK (n.d.c), 'NHK Kōhaku Utagassen Hisutorī [Kohaku Uta Gassen History]', *NHK*, Available online: http://www1.nhk.or.jp/kouhaku/history/ (accessed 4 February 2023c).

Nikkan Sports (2011), 'Arashi Utawanai Tōkyō Dōmu 90-Bu Gakkō No Sensei Ni [Arashi Do Not Sing. For 90 Minutes at the Tokyo Dome They Become School Teachers]', *Nikkan Sports*, Available online: https://www.nikkansports.

com/entertainment/news/p-et-tp0-20110519-777900.html (accessed 21 February 2023).

Nikkan Sports (2019a), 'NHK Ga Arashi No Katsudō Kyūshi o Sokuhō, Nittere & Fuji Ga Saisoku [NHK's Breaking News of Arashi's Hiatus, NTV & Fuji Are the Fastest]', *Nikkan Sports*, Available online: https://www.nikkansports.com/entertainment/news/201901270000659.html (accessed 18 February 2023).

Nikkan Sports (2019b), '62-Nen Sōgyō Janī Kitagawasan to Janīzu No Ayumi [Founded in 1962 History of Johnny Kitagawa and Johnny's]', *Nikkan Sports*, Available online: https://www.nikkansports.com/entertainment/news/201906210001254.html (accessed 4 February 2023).

Nikkan Sports (2022), 'Papa Ni Naru Aiba Masaki Otōsan Wa Konna Kanjinandarouna Kōhai He No Tanpure Erabi de Issoku Hayaku Jikkan [Masaki Aiba, Who Will Become a Father, Tells a Junior "I Wonder If My Father Is like This"]', *Nikkan Sports*, Available online: https://www.nikkansports.com/entertainment/news/202208310000956.html (accessed 27 February 2023).

Nikkan Sports (2023), 'Sakurai Shō Dai 1-Shi Ga Tanjō Itashimashita Arashi Menbā Ga Papa Ni Naru No Wa 3 Hitome 21-Nen Ni Ippan Josei to Kekkon [Sakurai Sho's First Child Was Born. The Third Arashi Member to Become a Father Married to a Non-Celebrity Woman in 2021]', *Nikkan Sports*, Available online: https://www.nikkansports.com/entertainment/news/202302150001042.html (accessed 27 February 2023).

Nippon Television Network Corporation (n.d.), '24Jikan Terebi [24 Hour Tv]', *24Hour Television*, Available online: https://www.ntv.co.jp/24h/ (accessed 11 February 2023).

Nippon Terebi News (2023), 'King & Prince Shindereragāru Wo Mirion Ni Hirogaru Oi Derera Genshō [The Phenomenon of Oi Derella Spreads. King & Prince's Cinderella Girl Way to the Million', *Yahoo! Japan News*, Available online: https://news.yahoo.co.jp/articles/7a8536b43d557003a7f14b7905a97119753c40b5 (accessed 5 May 2023).

Nornes, A. M. and F. Yukio (2021), *The Japan/America Film Wars*, ed. M. N. Abé and Y. Fukushima, London: Routledge.

Notani, S. (2023), 'Kōrei Risō No Jōshi Rankingu 7-Nen Renzoku de 1-i Wa? [The Annual Ideal Boss Ranking, Who Is First for 7 Years in a Row?]', *IT Media Business*, Available online: https://www.itmedia.co.jp/business/articles/2302/06/news135.html (accessed 10 March 2023).

Nye, J. (2011), 'Nye: A Reviving Japan?', *CNN.com*, Available online: https://globalpublicsquare.blogs.cnn.com/2011/11/15/nye-a-reviving-japan/ (accessed 17 February 2023).

Oguma, E. (2002), *A Genealogy of 'Japanese' Self-Images*, Melbourne: Trans Pacific Press.

Oi, M. (2019), 'Johnny Kitagawa: Japanese Boy Band Mogul Dies at 87', *BBC*, Available online: https://www.bbc.com/news/world-asia-48927331 (accessed 1 April 2023).

Okamoto, K. (2023), 'Mediade Wa Kesshite Kataranakatta Boku No Ima Genzai No Shōjikina Kimochi Wo Ohanashi Shimasu [I Will Talk Honestly about Things That I Could Not Talk about in the Media]', *YouTube*, Available online: https://www.youtube.com/watch?v=zGotapV0COM (accessed 13 May 2023).

Olson, K. R. (2006), 'A Literature Review of Social Mood', *Journal of Behavioral Finance*, 7 (4): 193–203.

Ongaku Natalie (2023), 'Snow Man Ga Takizawa Hideaki He Seichōshita Bokutachi Wo Mite Hoshī, Tsuittā Ni Kansō Wo [Snow Man Dedicate the Following Grateful Words to Takizawa Hideaki on Twitter: We Want You to See Us Grown Up]', *Yahoo! Japan News*, Available online: https://news.yahoo.co.jp/articles/42c1c265a6 7c09769213cd78020a0a4b424328d0 (accessed 6 April 2023).

Onishi, Z. (2021), 'King & Prince Kokuminteki Aidorugurūpu' He Maishin! SMAPra to Onaji Shiren Wo Norikoete [King & Prince Ushes Forward to Become a National Idol Group! Overcoming the Same Trials as SMAP and Others]', *Enta Mega*, Available online: https://entamega.com/59414 (accessed 24 February 2023).

Oricon ME Inc (n.d.), 'Oricon Ranking', *Oricon*, Available online: https://www.oricon.co.jp/rank/ (accessed 10 February 2023).

Oricon News (2011a), 'SMAP Tokuban Ni "Marching J" Shūketsu! Hisai-Chi Ni Egao No Ēru Okuru ["Marching J" Gathered in SMAP Special Program! Sending Smiles and Cheers to the Disaster Region]', *Oricon News*, Available online: https://www.oricon.co.jp/news/86232/full/ (accessed 21 February 2023).

Oricon News (2011b), 'Arashi "Nippon No Arashi Pokettoban" Ga Hatsubai Yokka de 20 Man Koe Kotoshi Saikou No Shukanuriage Wo Kiroku [The Book of Arashi "The Arashi of Japan Pocket Edition" Sells More than 200000 in Four Days Getting This Year Record of Higher Weekly Sales]', *Oricon News*, Available online: http://www.oricon.co.jp/news/ranking/88340/full/ (accessed 18 February 2023).

Oricon News (2015), 'Dai 8-Kai Koibito Ni Shitai Dansei Yūmeijin Rankingu [8th Ranking of Male Celebrities Desired as Lovers]', *Oricon News*, Available online: https://www.oricon.co.jp/special/47669/ (accessed 4 March 2023).

Oricon News (2016), 'Janīzu No Ima Yakyū Taikai Kara Mieta Kessoku [The Solidarity Seen from Johnny's Baseball Tournament]', *Oricon News*, Available online: https://www.oricon.co.jp/news/2070277/full/ (accessed 3 March 2023).

Oricon News (2018), 'Kinpuri Iwahashi Genki, 11 Tsuki Shojun Kara Katsudō Kyūshi He Panikku Shōgai No Chiryō Sennen. Kanarazu Modotte Kimasu [King

& Prince's Iwahashi Genki to Go on Hiatus from Early November to Focus on Treatment for Panic Disorder. He Says He'll Definitely Come Back]', *Oricon News*, Available online: https://www.oricon.co.jp/news/2122295/full/ (accessed 24 February 2023).

Oricon News (2019a), 'Nishikido Ryo, Kanjani∞ Dattai & Janizu Jimusho Wo 9 Gatsumatsu Taisho. Zenin Ga Manshin Sōi No Jōtai [Nishikido Ryo Leaves Kanjani∞ and Retires from Johnny's Jimusho at the End of September. All Members Are Hurt by the Situation]', *Oricon News*, Available online: https://www.oricon.co.jp/news/2143818/full/ (accessed 1 April 2023).

Oricon News (2019b), 'Kinpuri Hirano Shō Vivi Kokuhōkyū Ikemen Rankingu Dentōiri [King & Prince's Hirano Sho Enters ViVi's National Treasure-Level Handsome Man Ranking Hall of Fame]', *Oricon News*, Available online: https://www.oricon.co.jp/news/2149157/full/ (accessed 24 February 2023).

Oricon News (2021), 'Danjo Betsu Risō No Kōhai Rankingu [Ranking of Ideal Juniors by Gender]', *Oricon News*, Available online: https://www.oricon.co.jp/special/56084/3/ (accessed 10 March 2023).

Oricon News (2022a), 'King & Prince de Ichiban Osharena Menbā Wa? Dēto-Fuku Kōde de Taiketsu, Masakano Kappa Kōde Mo [King & Prince Which Member Is the Most Stylish? A Showdown in Date Outfit, and the Unexpected Kappa Outfit]', *Oricon News*, Available online: https://www.oricon.co.jp/news/2228557/full/ (accessed 10 March 2023).

Oricon News (2022b), 'Danjo Betsu Risō No Kōhai Rankingu 2022 [Ranking of Ideal Juniors by Gender 2022]', *Oricon News*, Available online: https://www.oricon.co.jp/special/58609/2/ (accessed 10 March 2023).

Oricon News (2022c), 'King & Prince Saishin-Saku Tsukiyomi/ Irodori Ga Mirion Toppa, Konnendo-Hatsu No Shingurumirion Tassei [King & Prince Latest Work Tsukiyomi/Irodori Has Surpassed the Million Mark, Achieving the First Million Single Sales This Year]', *Oricon News*, Available online: https://www.oricon.co.jp/news/2259455/full/ (accessed 31 March 2023).

Oricon News (2023a), 'Dai 16-Kai Josei Ga Erabu Koibito Ni Shitai Yūmeijin Rankingu [16th Ranking of Celebrities That Women Want to Have as Lovers]', *Oricon News*, Available online: https://www.oricon.co.jp/special/62337/ (accessed 4 March 2023).

Oricon News (2023b), 'King & Prince, 3-Shūkan-Buri Ni Eizō 3 Bumon Dōji 1-i [King & Prince Simultaneous Number 1 in 3 Video Categories for the First Time in 3 Weeks]', *Oricon News*, Available online: https://www.oricon.co.jp/news/2268016/full/ (accessed 24 February 2023).

Oricon News (2023c), 'King & Prince Saishin Shinguru Ga Deirīshinguru 1-i Konnendo Saikō Hatsu Shū Uriage 85.0 Man-Mai o Kiroku [King & Prince's Latest

Single Ranked Number 1 on the "Daily Singles" Selling 850,000 Copies in the First
Week a Record of the Year]', *Oricon News*, Available online: https://www.oricon.
co.jp/news/2268926/full/ (accessed 24 February 2023).

Oricon News (2023d), 'King & Prince Hatsu Shū Uriage 52.8 Man-Mai de Eizō 3
Bumon 1-i Shijō 2-Kumi-Me No 2-Saku Renzoku Hatsu Shū Uriage 50 Man-Mai
Koe [King & Prince First Week Sales of 528,000 Copies, Number 1 in the 3 Video
Divisions Second Work in History to Exceed 500,000 Copies in the First Week]',
Oricon News, Available online: https://www.oricon.co.jp/news/2273449/ (accessed
31 March 2023).

Oricon News (2023e), 'Kis-My-Ft 2 Kitayama Hiromitsu, Gurūpu Sotsugyō & Janīzu
Jimusho Taisho e Menbā & Fan e Kansha [Kis-My-Ft2 Hiromitsu Kitayama to
Graduate from Group & Leave Johnny's Office. He Thanks to Members and Fans]',
Oricon News, Available online: https://www.oricon.co.jp/news/2276977/full/
(accessed 28 August 2023).

Ota, S. (2020), 'Yamashita Tomohisa Ga Janizu Wo Yamerushikanakatta Hontō No
Riyū Takizawa Hideaki, Dentō, California [The Real Reason Yamashita Tomohisa
Had No Option but to Resign from Johnny's, Takizawa Hideaki, Tradition,
California]', *Bunshun Online*, Available online: https://bunshun.jp/articles/-/41595
(accessed 1 April 2023).

Pagliassotti, D., K. Nagaike and M. McHarry (2013), 'Editorial: Boys' Love Manga
Special Section', *Journal of Graphic Novels & Comics*, 4 (1): 1–8.

Pastukhov, D. (2022), 'Music Market Focus: Japan', *Soundcharts Blog*, Available
online: https://soundcharts.com/blog/japan-music-market-overview (accessed
10 February 2023).

Pflugfelder, G. M. (2012), 'The Nation-State, the Age/Gender System, and the
Reconstitution of Erotic Desire in Nineteenth-Century Japan', *The Journal of Asian
Studies*, 71 (4): 963–74.

PR Times (2011), 'Himitsunoarashichan Daininki Kikaku Manekinfaibu Dai 3-Dan
No Tōhyō Wa 3 Tsuki 7-Nichi (Tsuki) Sutāto! Anata No Ichi-Pyō Ga Arashi No
Unmei Wo Kimeru!! [Himitsu No Arashi-Chan! Voting for the Third Popular
Project Mannequin Five Will Start on March 7 (Monday)! Your Vote Will Decide
Arashi's Fate!!]', *PR Times*, Available online: https://prtimes.jp/main/html/
rd/p/000000011.000003065.html (accessed 10 March 2023).

Rankingu! (2023), 'Wakate Johnny's Ikemen TOP 10 [Top 10 of Johnny's Handsome
Men]', *Yahoo! Japan*, Available online: https://article.yahoo.co.jp/detail/
fab7f25196e7e9d1185573b899dcb3a4b4d20da3 (accessed 8 May 2023).

Real Sound (2018), 'King & Prince Jinguuji Yūta, Kokuminteki Kareshi No Imyō Ni
Sogū Hōyōryoku Gurūpunai de Hanatsu Sonzaikan Ni Semaru [King & Prince's
Jinguji Yuta's Ability to Match the Nickname of National Boyfriend Unleashes

within the Group]', *Real Sound*, Available online: https://realsound.jp/2018/10/post-261688.html (accessed 4 March 2023).

Real Sound (2019), 'Arashi, Kōshiki Yūchūbu Channeru Totsujo Kaisetsu & Sutorīmingu Kaikin! Genzai Wa 5-Kyoku Ga Kōkaichū [Arashi, Official YouTube Channel Suddenly Opened & Streamed! 5 Songs Are Currently Available]', *Real Sound*, Available online: https://realsound.jp/tech/2019/10/post-428248.html (accessed 28 February 2023).

Real Sound (2021), '2021-Nen Shinki Kaisetsu Channeru Tōrokushasū Rankingu TOP 10-Chū 4 Channeru Ga Janīzu Jimusho Kara [2021 Ranking of the Most Subscribers to New Channels. 4 out of the Top 10 Are Channels from Johnny's Jimusho]', *Real Sound*, Available online: https://realsound.jp/tech/2021/12/post-936752.html (accessed 25 February 2023).

Real Sound (2023), 'King & Prince Fan Ni Yoru "oi Derera" Undō No Seika 5 Toshikoshi de Debyū Shinguru "Shinderera Gāru" Mirion Sērusu Tassei [King & Prince, the Result of the "Oiderella" Movement by Fans Make Their Debut Single "Cinderella Girl" Achieves Million Sales after 5 Years]', *Yahoo! Japan News*, Available online: https://news.yahoo.co.jp/articles/063e2f9090f2b82596fb86c606d93206af1787db (accessed 14 May 2023).

Recording Industry Association of Japan (2000), 'A Brief Description of the Japanese Recording Industry 2000', Tokyo.

Recording Industry Association of Japan (2001), 'The Recording Industry in Japan Statistics, Analysis, Trends, RIAJ Yearbook 2001', Tokyo.

Recording Industry Association of Japan (2004), 'The Recording Industry in Japan Statistics, Analysis, Trends 2004', Tokyo.

Recording Industry Association of Japan (2006), 'Statistics Analysis Trends The Recording Industry in Japan 2006', Tokyo.

Recording Industry Association of Japan (2007), 'The Recording Industry in Japan 2007', Tokyo.

Recording Industry Association of Japan (2008), 'The Recording Industry in Japan 2008', Tokyo.

Recording Industry Association of Japan (2009), 'The Recording Industry in Japan 2009', Tokyo.

Recording Industry Association of Japan (2010), 'Statistics Trends The Recording Industry in Japan 2010', Tokyo.

Recording Industry Association of Japan (2011), 'Statistics Trends The Recording Industry in Japan 2011', Tokyo.

Recording Industry Association of Japan (2012), 'Statistics Trends The Recording Industry in Japan 2012', Tokyo.

Recording Industry Association of Japan (2015), 'Statistics Trends The Recording Industry in Japan 2015', Tokyo.

Recording Industry Association of Japan (2016), 'Statistics Trends The Recording Industry in Japan 2016', Tokyo.

Recording Industry Association of Japan (2017), 'Statistics Trends Overview of Production of Recordings and Digital Music Sales in 2016', Tokyo.

Recording Industry Association of Japan (2018), 'The Record', Tokyo.

Recording Industry Association of Japan (2020), 'Statistics Trends The Recording Industry in Japan 2020', Tokyo.

Recording Industry Association of Japan (2021), 'Statistics Trends RIAJ Year Book 2021', Tokyo.

Recording Industry Association of Japan (2022), 'Statistics Trends RIAJ Yearbook 2022', Tokyo.

Recording Industry Association of Japan (2023a), 'Statistics Trends RIAJ YEAR BOOK', Tokyo.

Recording Industry Association of Japan (2023b), 'Ātisuto Obu Za Iyā (Hōgaku Bumon) [Artist of the Year (Japanese Music Category)]', *The Japan Gold Disc Award*, Available online: https://www.golddisc.jp/award/37/best-artist01.html (accessed 31 March 2023).

Ronald (2021), 'V6 Disbands, While Ken Miyake Starts Anew', *Arama! Japan*, Available online: https://aramajapan.com/news/v6-disbands-while-ken-miyake-starts-anew/115765/ (accessed 1 April 2023).

Ryall, J. (2019), 'How a Gay Student's Suicide after Being Outed Is Helping Japan's LGBT Community Speak up', *South China Morning Post*, Available online: https://www.scmp.com/news/asia/east-asia/article/3007284/how-gay-students-suicide-after-being-outed-helping-japans-lgbt (accessed 15 October 2022).

Said, E. W. (1985), 'Orientalism Reconsidered', *Cultural Critique* (1): 89–107. https://doi.org/10.2307/1354282.

Said, E. W. (2003), *Orientalism*, New York: Penguin Books.

Saito, T. (2020), 'Media Tayōka Jidai No 20-Dai to Terebi [Television and the Twenties Era of Media Diversification]', *NHK Broadcasting Culture Research Institute*, Available online: https://www.nhk.or.jp/bunken/research/domestic/pdf/20200201_11.pdf (accessed 1 February 2020).

Sakai, M. (2005), 'Aidoru Sangyō-Sono Keizaitokusei to Shakaiseido, Bunseki to Seisaku', Working Paper, Institution Project-P. l, Available online: http://www.ppp.am/p-project/japanese/paper/sakai-paper.pdf.

Sakai, Y. (2020), 'The Takarazuka Revue and the Depiction of Gender Stereotypes since 1914', *Digital Humanities and Japanese History*, Available online: https://dh.japanese-history.org/2020-spring-women-in-japanese-history/the-takarazuka-revue-and-the-depiction-of-gender-stereotypes-since-1914/ (accessed 15 October 2022).

Sakashita, T. (2020), 'Tegoshi Yuya Ga Janizu Taisho Yurusanai to Okoru Fan, Sorezore No Riyū [The Reasons of Fans Not Forgiving That Tegoshi Yuya Retires from Johnny's]', *J-Cast News*, Available online: https://www.j-cast. com/2020/06/19388352.html?p=all (accessed 1 April 2023).

Sanae Toriko (2023), 'Kinpuri Taisho-Gumi Wo Ōen Suru Daikigyō Ni Hakujukassai … Aisare-Ryoku No Hirano Shō-Tachi Wa Taishogo Mo Antai Ka [A Round of Applause for the Large Companies That Support King & Prince's Members Who Leave … Are the Beloved and Powerful Hirano Sho and Others Safe after Leaving?]', *YouTube*, Available online: https://www.youtube.com/watch?v=sXQ NESn2vFs&list=PLskrcg1Z9o4z0Qe8Ev_V-o78lCFv9vhYs&index=14 (accessed 9 May 2023).

Sanpo.com (2004), 'Kōbe Ni Shikkari Kizama Reta J - FRIENDS No Ashiato [The Footprints of J-FRIENDS Firmly Carved in Kobe]', *Sanpo.com*, Available online: https://web.archive.org/web/20040414055720/http://www.sanspo.com/geino/top/ gt200403/gt2004031902.html (accessed 21 February 2023).

Sansupo (2019), 'Janī Kitagawasan, Entame No Dīenuē Chichi Mo Mizora Hibari No LA Kōen Assen [Johnny Kitagawa's Entertainment DNA. His Father Was Mediator in Misora Hibari's LA Performance]', *Sansupo*, Available online: https://www. sanspo.com/article/20190710-ZTPYOH7RWZIOBCTIVNSTHGST2Q/ (accessed 3 February 2023).

Sato, B. H. (2003), *The New Japanese Woman: Modernity, Media, and Women in Interwar Japan*, Durham: Duke University Press.

Schilling, M. (2019), 'Johnny Kitagawa: Power, Abuse, and the Japanese Media Omerta', *Variety*, Available online: https://variety.com/2019/film/asia/johnny-kitagawa-power-abuse-japanese-media-omerta-1203271575/ (accessed 4 February 2023).

Schmidt-Hori, S. (2009), 'The New Lady-in-Waiting Is a Chigo: Sexual Fluidity and Dual Transvestism in a Medieval Buddhist Acolyte Tale', *Japanese Language and Literature*, 43 (2): 383–423.

Sekiguchi, Y. (2021), 'Arashi Wa Aidoru o Koete Ikiru Daigomi Ni Natta. Arashi's Diary Voyage Saishūbanashi Ga Utsushidasu Tabi No Shūchakuchi [Arashi Has Gone beyond Being an Idol and Has Become the Real Pleasure of Living. The End of the Journey Reflected in the Final Episode of Arashi's Diary Voyage]', *Banger*, Available online: https://www.banger.jp/drama/54546/ (accessed 24 February 2023).

Senju, K. (2017), 'Moto SMAP Kusanagi Tsuyoshi Ga Kako Ni Okoshita Zenra Deisui Wo Furikaeru [Looking Back on Former SMAP Kusanagi Tsuyoshi's Past Naked

Drunkenness]', *Excite News*, Available online: https://www.excite.co.jp/news/
article/E1483578910102/?p=2 (accessed 23 February 2023).

Shamoon, D. (2009), 'Misora Hibari and the Girl Star in Postwar Japanese Cinema',
Journal of Women in Culture & Society, 35 (1): 131.

Shūkan Bunshun Henshubu (2023a), 'Kore Wo Gaman Shinai to Urenaikara Ei
BBC Ga Hōjita Janī Kitagawa-Shi No Sei Kagai Moto Janīzu Junia Ga Kaodashi
de Shōgeki Kokuhaku [If You Don't Put up with This, You Won't Sell Johnny
Kitagawa's Sexual Assault Reported by British BBC Former Johnny's Junior
Shocking Confession]', *Bunshun Online*, Available online: https://bunshun.jp/
articles/-/61200 (accessed 25 March 2023).

Shūkan Bunshun Henshūbu (2023b), 'Kei 15-Kai Wa Atta Hajimete No Jitsumei
Kaodashi Kokuhatsu Moto Janīzu Jr. Okamoto Kauanshi Ga Kataru Janī
Kitagawashi Seikagai [There Were a Total of 15 Times. The First Accusation That
Uses the Real Name and Face. Former Johnny's Jr. Okamoto Kowan Talks about
Johnny Kitagawa's Sexual Assault]', *Bunshun Online*, Available online: https://
bunshun.jp/articles/-/61911 (accessed 4 April 2023).

Shūkan Josei PRIME (2019), 'Janī Kitagawasan Seikyo, Bēru Ni Tsutsuma Reta
Oitachi to Dansei Aidoru Ninchi Sa Seta Kōseki [Johnny Kitagawa's Death. A
Veiled Upbringing and Achievements That Made Male Idols Known]', *Shukan
Josei PRIME*, Available online: https://www.jprime.jp/articles/-/15591 (accessed
4 February 2023).

Shūkan Josei PRIME (2023a), 'Janīzu Jr. 22-Sai Teinensei No Tekiyōsha Wo Sūnin to
Akasu Mo, Jissai No Taishosha Wa 10-Dai Ga 10-Ri Ijō No Fuon [The Johnny's
Jr 22-Year-Old Retirement System Causes Unrest. Numerous People Have Been
Discharged in Their Teens]', *Yahoo! Japan News*, Available online: https://news.
yahoo.co.jp/articles/497b20bbcf1d2058765bf3b2c36e3288441166c9 (accessed
3 April 2023).

Shūkan Josei Prime (2023b), 'King & Prince Takahashi Kaito Ga "oshare Kurippu" de
Oetsu Mo Majie Gōkyū. Ichibu Tiara Ga Inbō-Ron o Buchi Age Bōsō-Chū "Kaito
Ga Watashitachi Ni Tasuke o Motomete Iru" [King & Prince Kaito Takahashi
Cries and Sobs with "Oshare Clip". Some Tiara Raise Conspiracy Theories and Cry
out That Kaito Is Asking for Help]', *Shūkan Josei Prime*, Available online: https://
www.jprime.jp/articles/-/27522 (accessed 10 April 2023).

Smart Flash (2022), 'Kyoku Tsukaezu Chijōha Kara Kieru IMPACTors Zenin
Taisho de Matsu Ubara No Michi Soredemo Tomaranu Janizu Jinzai Ryūshutsu
No Shinkokusa [The Songs Disappear from the Terrestrial Broadcast A
Road of Thorns Awaits for Members of IMPACTors ... Still the Exhibition of
Johnny's Talents Do Not Stop]', *Yahoo News*, Available online: https://news.

yahoo.co.jp/articles/f195d1464d893624d6e556203057fd7621e272ee (accessed 1 April 2023).

Smith, A. D. (2007), 'Nations in Decline? The Erosion and Persistence of Modern National Identities', in M. Young, E. Zuelow and A. Sturm (eds), *Nationalism in a Global Era: The Persistence of Nations*, 16–29, New York: Routledge.

Sponichi Annex (2004), 'Hisaisha Ni Yūki Wo … Janīzu Yakyū Taikai [Giving Courage to Disaster Victims … Johnny's Baseball Tournament]', *Sponichi Annex*, Available online: http://www.sponichi.co.jp/entertainment/kiji/2004/11/13/02.html (accessed 3 March 2023).

Sponichi Annex (2019), 'Janī-San No Ayumi Chichi Wa Puroyagu Kyūdan Mane, Yakyū Chīmu Kara 4-Ri Erabi Shodai Janīzu Kessei [Johnny's History. Father Manages a Professional Baseball Team, Selects Four Members from the Baseball Team, and Forms the First Johnny's]', *Sponichi Annex*, Available online: https://www.sponichi.co.jp/entertainment/news/2019/07/10/kiji/20190710s00041000008000c.html (accessed 3 February 2023).

Sponichi Annex (2022), 'Kinpuri-Gan, Hirano, Jinguuji No 3-Ri Ga Dattai, Taisho Rainen 5 22 De … kujūnoketsudan. Nagase, Takahashi de Katsudō Keizoku [King & Prince's Kishi, Hirano, and Jinguji Withdraw from the Group, Leaving on May 22 Next Year … a Painful Decision. Nagase and Takahashi Continue Their Activities]', *Sponichi Annex*, Available online: https://www.sponichi.co.jp/entertainment/news/2022/11/04/kiji/20221104s00041000555000c.html (accessed 24 February 2023).

Stickland, L. R. (2004), 'Gender Gymnastics: Performers, Fans and Gender Issues in the Takarazuka Revue of Contemporary Japan', *Stickland, Leonie Rae*, PhD thesis, Murdoch: Murdoch University, Available online: https://researchrepository.murdoch.edu.au/view/author/SticklandLeonie.html.

Stoneman, J. (2009), 'Between Monks: Saigyō's Shukke, Homosocial Desire, and Japanese Poetry', *Japanese Language and Literature*, 43 (2): 425–52.

Sugiyama, M. (2020), 'Kusanagi Tsuyoshi, Deisui Zenra Sōdō Wo Kaiko Jinseite No Wa Wakarimasenne Osake Kaikin No Kikkake Mo Kataru [Kusanagi Tsuyoshi Recalls His Drunken Naked Riot "I Didn't Know What Life Was" and Talks about Quitting Alcohol]', *RRB Today*, Available online: https://www.rbbtoday.com/article/2020/10/03/182675.html (accessed 21 February 2023).

Suzuki, S. (2005), *Nihon No Bunka Nashonarizumu [Japan's Cultural Nationalism]*, Tokyo: Heibonsha.

Takahashi, F. (2019), 'Arashi, Katsudō Kyūshi Wo Kisha Kaiken de Hōkoku. Namidagumu Ōno Satoshi Wa Arashide Yokatta. Aiba Masaki Kizuna Wa Tsuyoku Natteru [Arashi Announces Hiatus at Press Conference. Ohno Satoshi,

Who Was in Tears, Said, Arashi Was Good. Masaki Aiba Says That Their Bond Is Getting Stronger]', *Huffington Post*, Available online: https://www.huffingtonpost.jp/entry/arashi-press-c_jp_5c5d8dd6e4b0974f75b3d78f (accessed 25 February 2023).

Takahashi, M. (2022), 'Jōshi Ya Senpai Ni Natte Hoshī 30-Dai No Janīzutarento Rankingu! Dai 1-i Wa Kamenashi Kazuya [Ranking Od Johnny's Talent in Their 30s That I Want to Be My Boss or Senior! The First Place Is Kamenashi Kazuya]', *Netorabo*, Available online: https://news.yahoo.co.jp/articles/33652f06d77d12f276 183b12a2a46304b7dbb014 (accessed 10 March 2023).

Takizawa, H. (2023), 'Hideaki Takizawa (@h_Takizawa386)', *Twitter*, Available online: https://twitter.com/h_Takizawa386/status/1638073017514471424/photo/1 (accessed 1 April 2023).

Takō, W. (2023), 'Hirano Shō to Nagase Ren Ga Janī-Shi No Manshon De … Kauan Okamoto-Shi (26) No Seikagai Kokuhatsu to Janīzu-Nai No Gorioshi Futatsu No Jijitsu Kara Wakitatte Shimau. Fan No Fuan to Wa. [Fans' Anxiety behind the Two Truths Regarding Okamoto Kowan's (26) Sexual Assault Accusation and Johnny's Pushing. Hiirano Sho and Nagase Ren at Johnny's Apartment …]', *Bunshun Online*, Available online: https://bunshun.jp/articles/-/62357 (accessed 22 April 2023).

Talent Power Ranking (2023a), 'Tarento Pawā Rankingu [Talent Power Ranking]', *Talent Power Ranking*, Available online: https://tpranking.com/ (accessed 5 February 2023).

Talent Power Ranking (2023b), '10 ~ 20-Dai No Wakate Janīzu Jimusho Shozoku Tarento No Saishin Rankingu Wo Happyō! [Announcing the Latest Ranking of Young Johnny's Jimusho Talents in Their Teens and Twenties!]', *Talent Power Ranking*, Available online: https://tpranking.com/young-johnnys (accessed 16 April 2023).

Talent Power Ranking (2023c), '2023-Nenban Z Sedai Ni Shijisareteiru Dansei Tarento & Josei Tarento TOP 10! [2023 Edition of the Top 10 Male Talents and Female Talents Supported by Generation Z!]', *Talent Power Ranking*, Available online: https://tpranking.com/generationz-2023-02?page=2 (accessed 16 April 2023).

Tanaka, Y. (1995), *Contemporary Portraits of Japanese Women*, Westport: Greenwood Publishing Group.

Tatsuta, A. (2010), 'Kokuminteki Aidoru Ga, Honmono No Ii Otoko Ni Naru Hi [The Day That the National Idols Become Real Good Men]', *GQ Japan*, June: 36–41.

TBS News Dig (2023), 'Janīzu Jimusho Ga Kaiken Shin Shachō No Higashiyama Noriyuki-Shi, Jurī-Shi, Inoharayoshihiko-Shi-Ra Ga Shusseki [Johnny's Office Held a Press Conference with New President Noriyuki Higashiyama, Julie,

Yoshihiko Inohara and Others Attending]', *YouTube*, Available online: https://www.youtube.com/watch?v=uXQMe58ne04 (accessed 7 September 2023).

The First Times (2022), 'Ichiban Osharena No Wa Dare? King & Prince, Kinpuru de Dēto-Fuku Kōdinēto Taiketsu [Who Is the Most Fashionable? King & Prince, a Confrontation of Date Clothes Coordinate in Kinpuru]', *The First Times*, Available online: https://www.thefirsttimes.jp/news/0000093344/ (accessed 10 March 2023).

The First Times (2023), 'King & Prince Tsukiyomi MV 1 Okukaisaisei Koe! Kinpurirashī Tiara (Fan) He No Kansha Mo [King & Prince Tsukiyomi MV over 100 Million Views! Appreciation for Kinpuri Tiara (Fans)]', *The First Times*, Available online: https://www.thefirsttimes.jp/news/0000258414/ (accessed 26 March 2023).

The Foreign Correspondents' Club of Japan (2023a), 'Predator – BBC Documentary on Johnny Kitagawa by Mobeen Azhar & Megumi Inman – YouTube', *The Foreign Correspondents' Club of Japan Official YouTube Channel*, Available online: https://www.youtube.com/watch?v=t2SisAVaS-w (accessed 24 March 2023).

The Foreign Correspondents' Club of Japan (2023b), 'Alleged Victim of Johnny Kitagawa Speaks Out', *YouTube*, Available online: https://www.youtube.com/watch?v=EoWwZpOZyyk (accessed 9 May 2023).

The Huffington Post (2014), 'Kokuritsukyōgijō, Tandoku Raibu Wo Okonatta No Wa Wazuka 6-Kumi Densetsu No Ongaku Ibento Wo Furikaeru [Only 6 Groups Performed Solo Concerts at the National Stadium. Looking Back on the Legendary Music Events]', *The Huffington Post*, Available online: https://www.huffingtonpost.jp/2014/05/31/kokuritsu-music_n_5422764.html (accessed 21 February 2023).

The Yomiuri Shimbun (2023), 'Ken Miyake, Ex-V6 Member to Leave Johnny & Associates', *The Japan News*, Available online: https://japannews.yomiuri.co.jp/culture/film-tv/20230221-92571/ (accessed 1 April 2023).

Thorn, M. (2004), 'Girls and Women Getting Out of Hand: The Pleasure and Politics of Japan's Amateur Comics Community', in K. Williams (ed), *Fanning the Flames: Fans and Consumer Culture in Contemporary Japan*, 169–88, New York: State University of New York.

TOBE (2023a), 'Message', *TOBE*, Available online: https://tobe-newstar.jp/ (accessed 1 April 2023).

TOBE (2023b), 'Artist', *TOBE*, Available online: https://tobe-official.jp/artists (accessed 28 August 2023).

Tokyo 2020 Candidate City (2011), 'Message, Concept', *Tokyo 2020 Candidate City*, Available online: http://www.tokyo2020.jp/jp/message/ (accessed 17 September 2012).

Tokyo Sports (2023), 'Sekuzo Kikuchi Fūma Ga Beikoku Mezasu Ātisuto Ni Mono Mōsu Kinpurifan Mō Hanpatsu [Sexy Zone's Kikuchi Fuma Makes a Statement about Artists Aiming for the United States. King & Prince Fans Responded

Vehemently]', *Yahoo! Japan News*, Available online: https://news.yahoo.co.jp/articles/d89217b75a6c1628406dbdae209024f41875290f (accessed 6 April 2023).

Toriyama, A. and D. Buist (2003), 'Okinawa's "Postwar": Some Observations on the Formation of American Military Bases in the Aftermath of Terrestrial Warfare', *Inter-Asia Cultural Studies*, 4 (3): 400–17.

Trend Magazine 50 (2023), 'Naze IMPACTors Taisho! Hontō No Riyū Wa Juri Shachō Ni Kirawareta Kara [Why IMPACTors Retire! The Real Reason Is Because They Are Hated by President Julie]', *Trend Magazine 50*, Available online: https://www.fukuoka-fa.com/impactors-taisyo/ (accessed 1 April 2023).

Trill (2023), 'Ikebo Da to Omou Wakate Janīzu Rankingu! 3-i Matsumura Hokuto, Yamada Ryōsuke, 2-i Meguro Ren, 1-i Wa? [Cool Young Johnny's Ranking! 3rd Place Matsumura Hokuto, Ryosuke Yamada, 2nd Place Meguro Ren, 1st Place?]', *Trill Trill*, Available online: https://trilltrill.jp/articles/3107424 (accessed 4 May 2023).

TV Asahi (2020), 'Yamashita Tomohisa (35) Ga Janizu Jimusho Wo Taisho [Yamashita Tomohisa (35) Leaves Johnny's Jimusho]', *Tereasa News*, Available online: https://news.tv-asahi.co.jp/news_society/articles/000198066.html (accessed 1 April 2023).

Ueno, H. and B. Dooley (2023), 'Japanese Talent Agency Admits Founder Preyed on Boys in Its Care', *The New York Times*, Available online: https://www.nytimes.com/2023/09/07/business/japan-boyband-sexual-abuse.html (accessed 6 September 2023).

Ui, Y. (2019), 'Janī Kitagawa Mizukara Ga Katatta Geinōshi Wo Kaeta Sūkina Jinsei [Johnny Kitagawa Himself Talked about the Life That Changed the History of Entertainment]', *Gendai Bussiness*, Available online: https://gendai.media/articles/-/65419 (accessed 3 February 2023).

UN Women (2023), 'Penal Code of 1908', *UN Women*, Available online: https://evaw-global-database.unwomen.org/fr/countries/asia/japan/1908/penal-code-1908 (accessed 12 May 2023).

Universal Music Japan (n.d.), 'NEWS – King & Prince', *Universal Music Japan*, Available online: https://www.universal-music.co.jp/king-and-prince/news/ (accessed 24 February 2023).

Uno, K. S. (1993), 'The Death of "Good Wife, Wise Mother"?', in A. Gordon (ed), *Postwar Japan as History*, 293–323, Los Angeles: University of California Press.

Upham, F. K. (1993), 'Unplaced Persons and Movements for Place', in A. Gordon (ed), *Postwar Japan as History*, 325–46, Los Angeles: University of California Press.

Valaskivi, K. (2013), 'A Brand New Future? Cool Japan and the Social Imaginary of the Branded Nation', *Japan Forum*, 25 (4): 485–504.

Viscomi, M. (2019), 'Nietzsche's Critique of Positivism. The Dialectical Unity of the Existent', in B. Pešić and P. Žitko (eds), *Existence and the One*, 367, Buenos Aires: Teseo.

Vivi (2020), 'Kokuhōkyū Ikemen Ankēto Kaishi! Rekidai No Rankingu Wo Furikaeri [The Questionnaire to the National Treasure-Level Handsome Man Begins! Looking Back on Past Rankings]', *ViVi*, Available online: https://www.vivi.tv/post146732/ (accessed 25 February 2023).

Vivi (2022), 'ViVi Kokuhōkyū Ikemen Happyō Chokuzen. Dentōiri Shita Rekidai No Ikementachi o Pureibakku [Just before the Announcement of ViVi's National Treasure Level Handsome Guy We Review the Men Who Entered the Hall of Fame]', *Vivi*, Available online: https://www.vivi.tv/post277942/ (accessed 24 February 2023).

Vodzoo (2021), 'Renzoku Dokyumentarī RIDE ON Taimu No Dōga Wo Haishin-Chū No Sābisu to Wa? [What Services Are Currently Delivering Videos of the Serial Documentary RIDE ON TIME?]', *Vodzoo*, Available online: https://www.vodzoo.com/av_contents/ride-on-time/ (accessed 24 February 2023).

Vogel, E. (1971), *Japan's New Middle Class: The Salary Man and His Family in a Tokyo Suburb*, Berkeley: University of California Press.

Web Japan (2000), 'Shingo Mama – What's Cool in Japan', *Web Japan*, Available online: https://web-japan.org/kidsweb/archives/cool/00-07-09/shingomama.html (accessed 11 March 2023).

Web The Television (2018), 'King & Prince Debyū Yume Wa Dekkaku Sekai e! Yorokobi No Kaiken Wo Zenbun Keisai [King & Prince's Debut, Their Dream Is Going Global. The Full Text of the Joyful Interview Is Posted]', *Web The Television*, Available online: https://thetv.jp/news/detail/134441/ (accessed 25 February 2023).

Web The Television (2023), 'King & Prince Hirano Shō, Fasshon Taiketsu de Otehon Ga Akazukin-Chan Shika Inai [Sho Hirano, There Is Only Little Red Riding Hood as a Role Model in the Fashion Confrontation]', *Web The Television*, Available online: https://thetv.jp/news/detail/1125413/ (accessed 10 March 2023).

West, M. D. (2006), *Secrets, Sex, and Spectacle: The Rules of Scandal in Japan and the United States*, Chicago: University of Chicago Press.

Williams, K. W. (2004), 'Introduction. Locating the Fans', in K. Williams (ed), *Fanning the Flames: Fans and Consumer Culture in Contemporary Japan*, 1–16, New York: State University of New York.

World Economic Forum (2023), 'Global Gender Gap Report 2023', Geneva.

Xu, J., G. Donnar and V. Kishore (2021), 'Internationalising Celebrity Studies: Turning towards Asia', *Celebrity Studies*, 12 (2): 175–85.

Yamada, M. (1999), *Parasaito Shinguru No Jidai*, Tokyo: Chikuma Shobo.

Yamamoto, U. (2022), 'Yabeeyo, Megane Wo Sentakki Ni Irete Aratchatta Yo! Kisha Ga Mokugeki Shita Jr Ni Taisuru Ko Janīshi No Ryōbosan No Yōna Ai Ima Janīzu Jimusho Ni Kakete Iru Mono [Oh No, I Put My Glasses in the Washing Machine and Washed Them! The Late Mr. Johnny's Dorm Mother-like Love for Jr. Witnessed by a Reporter. What Johnny's Jimusho Is Missing Now]', *Bunshun Online*, Available online: https://bunshun.jp/articles/-/59262?page=3 (accessed 25 March 2023).

Yano, C. R. (2003), *Tears of Longing. Nostalgia and the Nation in Japanese Popular Song*, Cambridge, MA: Harvard University Asia Center.

Yano, C. R. (2005), 'Covering Disclosures: Practices of Intimacy, Hierarchy, and Authenticity in a Japanese Popular Music Genre', *Popular Music and Society*, 28 (2): 193–205.

Yano, T. (2016), *Janizu to Nihon [Johnny's and Japan]*, Tokyo: Kodansha Gendai Shinsho.

Yeung, J. (2023), 'Head of Japan's Top Pop Agency Resigns after Admitting Late Founder Sexually Abused Minors for Decades', *CNN Business*, Available online: https://edition.cnn.com/2023/09/07/media/japan-kitagawa-agency-sexual-abuse-resignation-intl-hnk/index.html (accessed 6 September 2023).

Yoshino, K. (2005), *Cultural Nationalism in Contemporary Japan: A Sociological Enquiry*, London: Routledge.

Yoshioka, S. (2022), 'King & Prince Ga Kataru, Kokuminteki Aidoru to Natta Genzaichi [King & Prince Talks about Their Current Status as a National Idol]', *Nikkan SPA*, Available online: https://nikkan-spa.jp/1838363 (accessed 24 February 2023).

Yu, W. H. (2009), *Gendered Trajectories. Women, Work, and Social Change in Japan and Taiwan*, Stanford: Stanford University Press.

Yutura (2020), 'Arashi Ga Yūchūbu Channeru Tōrokushasū 300 Manri Tassei de Saisoku Kiroku Wo Kōshiñ kaisetsu Kara 346-Nichi [Arashi Breaks the Fastest Record by Reaching 3 Million YouTube Channel Subscribers 346 Days after Opening]', *Yutura*, Available online: https://yutura.net/news/archives/36392 (accessed 28 February 2023).

Ziembinski, B. (2015), 'Social Mood Revealed', in C. Bosco, E. Cambria, R. Damiano, V. Patti and P. Rosso (eds), *Emotion and Sentiment in Social and Expressive Media*, 35–50, Istanbul: Central Europe Workshop Proceedings.

Index

www.ingramcontent.com/pod-product-compliance
Lightning Source LLC
Chambersburg PA
CBHW062034270326
41929CB00014B/2427